MAGNIFICENT

OBSESSION

MAGNIFICENT
OBSESSION

BRIAN KIM

CHARISMA
HOUSE

trademarks registered in the United States Patent and Trademark Office by Biblica, Inc.™

Cover design by Lisa Rae McClure
Design Director: Justin Evans

Visit the author's website at www.antiochcenter.com.

Library of Congress Cataloging-in-Publication Data:
Kim, Brian, 1982-
  Magnificent obsession / by Brian Kim. -- First edition.
     pages cm
  Summary: "Crave a real encounter with God. True Christianity is an all-out commitment and devotion to Jesus. The first commandment, to love God with all of our heart, soul, mind, and strength, is not simply an invitation from God; it is a mandate placed on any person who calls himself a follower of Jesus. In this inspirational and thought-provoking book, Brian Kim explores what it means to lay down our lives, love Jesus wholeheartedly, and follow Him with abandon. The author will use Scriptures as well as personal stories from his own life to discuss various themes"-- Provided by publisher.
  ISBN 978-1-62136-563-1 (paperback) -- ISBN 978-1-62136-564-8 (e-book)
  1. Christian life. 2. Spirituality--Christianity. I. Title.
  BV4501.3.K544 2015
  248.4--dc23
                                                    2015009393

First edition

15 16 17 18 19 — 987654321
Printed in the United States of America

To my amazing children. I pray the truths in this book are modeled well for you and that you each love Jesus wholeheartedly, courageously, and with great joy all the days of your life.

CONTENTS

ACKNOWLEDGMENTS

Maureen Eha, Jevon Bolden, Leigh DeVore, and the many others at Charisma House Book Group who helped bring this book together, your patience, support, and skills were such an incredible contribution to this book and a blessing to me personally. I am deeply grateful.

To my wife, Grace, this book is yours. I couldn't have done it without you.

Special thanks to Mike Bickle, Lou Engle, and Dick Eastman, true heroes of faith in our day. Thank you for dreaming big dreams, living courageously, and inspiring young men and women to do the same. You have shown this generation a true witness of the worth and beauty of Jesus. You have modeled for us all what it looks like to make Jesus our magnificent obsession. My own life has been greatly impacted by your example, love, and encouragement—beyond what I can express in these few sentences—but as a son to men I consider spiritual fathers of this generation, I rise to call you "blessed" and thank you for your faithfulness in making the name of Jesus beautiful in the earth.

FOREWORD

A YOUNG LADY CALLED me from a city in the Himalayas. She had gone to be a worker among the unreached and unengaged people groups of that region. She had been playing her guitar and weeping in the middle of the night on the rooftop of her dwelling. I was so moved when she told me, "My tears were not just for the people who were without Christ; my heart was longing and aching for God."

Pondering her statement, I once again inwardly affirmed that truly worship and devotion to Jesus must be the main spring of all our Christian activity. How easily we can get bogged down in the grind of "to do" and lose the oil that sweetens life. How well I know this personally; I can live for a while off the adrenaline of vision and movement and conquering, but when the stillness comes, when I am left alone, I find something of a broken cistern in my heart rather than an artesian well.

I'm so encouraged that this first book by Brian Kim, who is like a son to me and one of my greatest encouragers, is about this subject: God, our magnificent obsession. I truly stand amazed at what God is doing with Brian and Grace and The Antioch Center for Training and Sending (ACTS). Young men and women are giving their lives to go to the hardest, darkest places to pray and serve among the unreached peoples, but I am finding something more precious than even the ACTS mission expansion. Those who go are carrying the inward flame of extravagant devotion to Christ. This was the flame of Hudson Taylor. This was the flame of Adoniram Judson. This was the flame of Amy Carmichael. This is the flame that must burn first in the final push toward giving Christ His inheritance among the nations.

I remember being in Washington, DC, with Brian, who was one of the key leaders with me as we established the Justice House of Prayer on Capitol Hill. Oh, I loved the contending prayer! My heavenly commission is to raise up a House of Prayer that contends with every other house that exalts itself against the knowledge and supremacy of Christ. Oh, I loved those "rumbles" as we thundered in intercession, even day and night, believing for justice for the unborn and the pregnant mother. Brian was one of the ringleaders of the "rumblers," and then something happened. It was drastic and sudden. He had an encounter with Jesus who was seeking his worship even more than his war. While reading Psalm 132 of David's longing for the presence of the Lord and his desire to set up a tabernacle of day and night worship on earth, as it is in heaven, Brian was apprehended with that same longing. My rumbler was becoming a lover. He spent his whole Christmas vacation alone seeking God rather than enjoying the pleasures of home and hearth. He was being set apart for love of God. As a matter of fact, many of our young men and women were also being drawn into a similar intimate encounter with Jesus. Brian's heart was being drawn to move to the International House of Prayer in Kansas City, Missouri, where my friend Mike Bickle had established a culture of bridal intimacy and day and night worship that was being cultivated over a period of many years. Brian was so dear to me, which made it somewhat painful to see him move to Kansas City, but inwardly I knew that this was the Lord's drawing. I had known that drawing as well. For years in Mott Auditorium in Pasadena, California, I would cry out in the nights for the Psalm 132 presence as David did, "I will not give sleep to my eyes or slumber to my eyelids, until I find a place for the LORD, a dwelling place for the Mighty One of Jacob" (v. 4, NKJV).

Brian followed that same Davidic song, and the sound has captured him ever since. Yes, he is still a "rumbler." Yes, he's on a great mission, but that mission is fueled by the song of the love for Christ that is now being heard in God's rising house of prayer in the earth! In every place this song will be heard, "Glory to the Righteous One"! In the mountains of the Himalayas, in the Buddhist high places of Tibet, in the Muslim strongholds of the Caucuses, to the war-riddled villages of Syria, Iraq, and Kurdistan, to the multiplied Hindu unreached people groups of the Gangetic Plain, to the ravaged regions of North Africa's deserts, and the impregnable outposts of Somalia, Yemen, and Oman—everywhere! The songs of our magnificent obsession will be heard.

The earth is returning to the ancient vocation of priesting before the throne of God. Priesting first, reigning second, this is the ancient paradigm. "One thing have I asked that I may seek that I may behold the beauty of the Lord and meditate in His sanctuary." Oh, if you could have asked David what was the main spring of his life, surely it must have been the glory of his kingly reign, surely it must have been victories in battles. He would have said, "You don't understand me. One thing have I asked." And God responded, "I HAVE FOUND DAVID! A man after My own heart!" This is positively immense that God would speak concerning man, "I have found David! I have found what I'm looking for. I have found a worshipper!"

Oh, I continually hear this great course correction in my own soul. I rejoice in the rumble and the war, but something inside me calls me back to Dillsburg, Pennsylvania, where soon after I was saved, I stepped into a little country church on the edge of town and God was there. There in my little trailer in the woods, for months, I could hardly bear the inward pain of spiritual desire and longing for God and His longing for me: "Jesus, ever let me find You in the woods of Dillsburg Pennsylvania, or the city of Pasadena, or wherever I am around the world. Bring me back to the main spring." May this be our cry, "Bring us back to the main spring."

I believe this book, *Magnificent Obsession*, and Brian's story can serve as a compass and maybe a course correction for the church's ministry and mission. As John Piper said, "Missions exists because worship doesn't." May every movement of God that springs from His people be fueled not just by boards and committees and planning sessions with strategies, but may the fuel of it be also as it was in ancient Antioch, "And they were fasting and ministering to the Lord and the Holy Spirit spoke." (See Acts 13:2.) May all of our action spring from the magnificent obsession.

I'm proud of you, Brian, my Psalm 132 man!

—Lou Engle
Founder, TheCall

FOREWORD

I LOVE THE TITLE of Brian Kim's book: *Magnificent Obsession*. It is surely what the Holy Spirit is emphasizing in the earth as we draw closer to the return of Jesus. When the Father promised to His Son that He would make all His enemies His footstool and give to Him the nations as His inheritance, He knew that His people would be "obsessed" with the majestic beauty of Jesus as the King of kings. The Holy Spirit is even now revealing Jesus's beauty to His people in the nations in this hour of history.

We long to see the fame of His name spread to all corners of the earth. I long to see the understanding and expression of Christianity shift from mere lip service and attendance card mentality to a whole-sale, no-turning-back obsession with the beauty and worth of Jesus Christ. As the return of Christ steadily approaches, we see an increase of darkness and rage of the evil one. Loving Jesus wholeheartedly is being challenged in a far more sophisticated and sinister way. But the promise of the Father to give His Son a glorious inheritance will surely come to pass. I believe the Holy Spirit will use this message, this call to love Jesus wholeheartedly, this appeal to a "magnificent obsession" to awaken the Western church in a new dimension. And I have great faith as I look out upon an army of men and women committed to righteousness, truth, and devotion to Jesus, walking in unashamed and courageous faith. Brian Kim is one of these burning ones in the earth.

I remember when I first met Brian. He was a scrappy, shaggy-haired, twentysomething who came to our missions base with high recommendation from my dear friend Lou Engle. Brian had spent a few years under Lou's mentorship, as his assistant and then in leadership with the prayer and justice initiatives they had embarked on in Washington, DC, Boston, and a few other areas. I remember being immediately struck by Brian's depth in the Word, humility, and clear leadership gift. In the following years I've often marveled at the powerful anointing of God on this young man's life. He served in various dimensions of leadership at our IHOPKC missions base and ultimately landed on our senior leadership team.

Over the years I have known Brian, I have found him to be uniquely courageous and yet lacking the self-promoting ambitions so prevalent in many young men and women in ministry. His authentic desire for God and bold, unrelenting commitment to the purposes of God in this generation have set him apart in many ways. He is wise beyond his years but walks in humility and seeks to honor his fathers and those who have gone before him. I have seen him take a strong, unrelenting stand for truth, and I have seen him weep in intercession and repentance. In short, Brian is the "real deal" and truly one of the most remarkable young leaders that I have ever met. He has been a great joy to me personally, and I anticipate great things to come as this young man continues to pursue the knowledge of God and courageous obedience to Jesus.

—MIKE BICKLE
DIRECTOR, INTERNATIONAL HOUSE OF
PRAYER, KANSAS CITY

PREFACE

I WOULD BE LYING if I pretended that as I endeavored to write this book I didn't, on numerous occasions, feel a sense of inadequacy. When it comes to the subject at hand, I would so much rather refer you to the books that have marked and shaped my own life, particularly the biographies of men and women of faith who have gone before this generation's time who lived lives of true, extravagant love—real heartsick obsession with Jesus. These individuals lived lives of true discipleship, obedience, and devotion, and their message is the same I seek to impart to all who read these pages—a message of such consuming fascination, radical obedience, and extravagant devotion to a beautiful and worthy God that it compels us to abandon all.

I am still a young man, so the vision of this magnificent obsession is still being formed in me. I dare not claim to own every truth contained in these pages as my daily reality. But I seek to inspire, provoke, and encourage a generation whose lives are the hinge of my children's future history.

In an age of so much gray, so much lackadaisical living and passionless existence, while so many on the earth are desperate for the message of peace and abundant life we claim to possess, I humbly present what I deem to be the answer for the question of purpose this generation cries out to receive. This book, *Our Magnificent Obsession*, is my humble contribution to the call of discipleship that the Holy Spirit continues to extend to the body of Christ.

I pray this call is evident through the pages of this book and that His Holy Spirit awakens your heart to greater depths of love, obedience, and devotion to Christ. Because He is, He was, and He forever will be worthy of our love and devotion. He is the beautiful One, the answer and the longing of every human heart. Until He returns, we will continue to ache for Him, the earth will continue to groan, and all will remain in a state gone awry.

May the words in this book provoke you. May a fire of passion for Jesus be kindled in your heart. And may your voice join the song of the Spirit and the bride in the end of ages, singing, "Come, Lord Jesus, come."

—Brian Kim

Chapter 1

THE MOST IMPORTANT QUESTION

When Jesus came into the region of Caesarea Philippi, He asked His disciples, saying, "Who do men say that I, the Son of Man, am?"

So they said, "Some say John the Baptist, some Elijah, and others Jeremiah or one of the prophets."

He said to them, "But who do you say that I am?"

Simon Peter answered and said, "You are the Christ, the Son of the living God."

Jesus answered and said to him, "Blessed are you, Simon Bar-Jonah, for flesh and blood has not revealed this to you, but My Father who is in heaven. And I also say to you that you are Peter, and on this rock I will build My church, and the gates of Hades shall not prevail against it. And I will give you the keys of the kingdom of heaven, and whatever you bind on earth will be bound in heaven, and whatever you loose on earth will be loosed in heaven."

Then He commanded His disciples that they should tell no one that He was Jesus the Christ.

—MATTHEW 16:13–20

W HO DO YOU say that I am?"

This question is haunting. It cuts deep. It's not a shallow, rhetorical question. Jesus isn't searching for a compliment here, asking His followers, "So, do you like Me?"

No, this question is the hinge on which your entire life's existence rests. Your purpose, your calling, your passion—the answer to this question defines you. You can't answer it quickly or lightly. You can't spout off the Christianese you might have learned so well in church. Every person must answer this question with gut-wrenching honesty and clarity.

When you were first saved, you probably would have answered this question with passionate sincerity, saying, "Jesus is my Savior," or, "Jesus is my rescuer." But as time wears on and we grow familiar with the lingo, the routine, and the religion, we often find that our original passion ebbs and flows. And if we're honest, we'd say our answer to that question becomes less and less clear with each passing season.

Furthermore, we find our churches and our generation offer alarmingly muddled responses to this question. The cutting clarity of the gospel has become instead a watered-down, palatable message of self-gratification—a hall pass for sloppy grace. You know how it goes: "Jesus heals. Jesus saves. Love wins. Do as you please."

But the question remains. Uncomfortably confrontational, gut-wrenchingly personal, it confronts us: "Who do you say that I am?"

ONE BRAVE RESPONSE

This was the question Jesus asked His disciples and closest friends who had traveled with Him for years. They had seen Him accomplish unbelievable signs and wonders. And on a day that seemed to be like any other normal day with Jesus—if you can reasonably call any day spent with Jesus normal!—they entered the region of Caesarea Philippi and paused with Jesus for an instructive moment.

They had no idea what was coming next.

First Jesus asked them, almost as if curious, "Who do men say that I, the Son of Man, am?" And the disciples responded as good Jewish boys would, spouting off the right answers, the usual suspects—John the Baptist, Jeremiah, Elijah, or some other prophet.

But then Jesus asked the all-important question: "Who do *you* say that I am?" Perhaps never before was so important a question asked by anyone.

I can only imagine the question took their breath away. Some probably panicked because honestly, they weren't exactly sure who He was. They knew He was important. He was obviously a man filled with the Spirit of God—how else could He perform such signs and miracles? And He was just so enjoyable to be around, so full of joy and magnetic charisma. He could awe a crowd with His stories, and He could baffle the arrogant religious leaders with His wisdom.

I'm sure many of Jesus's disciples were hopeful He was the promised Messiah, the one promised to deliver them from Roman occupation who would establish Jerusalem as the capital of the world, just as the Scriptures had prophesied. I'm guessing Simon the Zealot, the political radical, had followed Jesus at least in part for this reason. After all, what Israel really needed was a king, someone to rise in power and overthrow the oppression that had plagued the Jewish people for far too long.

But if any other disciples were at least hopeful Jesus was the Promised One, none but Peter dared to actually say it. You see, to say it—to actually admit to the belief that Jesus was the Messiah, the Savior of Israel—would be to blaspheme Jewish law. It would be the point of no return. Blasphemy was the ultimate no-no, punishable by death. So if anyone was going to answer that question—*really* answer that question—he had better be prepared to stake his life on the answer.

And it was Peter.

Peter, the endearingly rough-around-the-edges fisherman, was the one to break the tension in the air. He answered Jesus, maybe tentatively or maybe triumphantly, "You are the Christ, the Son of the living God."

What a statement. Pure faith.

I wish I could have heard his tone, the inflection of his voice. I imagine it communicated this: "You are the Messiah. You are more than any man has ever been. You are more than a prophet or a signpost. You are the Lord. You are God in flesh, come to rescue us all. You are the Christ, the Son of the Living God."

I want to live under this statement. It is the truest phrase the human heart has ever proclaimed.

A Personal Question

Now, the point of this interaction in Matthew 16 was not just to publicly proclaim the divine nature of Jesus. In fact, after Jesus confirmed Peter's confession as truth, He commanded the disciples not to tell anyone (v. 20). This speaks to something more raw and personal in Jesus's questioning. He wasn't asking the question just to make a point. He wanted to know their answer—just like He wants to know *our* answer. He's that relational, asking a personal question and looking for a personal answer from His friends.

How the disciples answered this question would ultimately determine everything about their future, their present, and even their past. In the same way, that question is the ultimate question all of God's creation must answer still today. Something significant—maybe even eternal—is at stake in how we answer it. What we think and believe about this Jewish man from Nazareth determines everything about our lives.

A. W. Tozer, in his book *Knowledge of the Holy*, powerfully states this reality:

> What comes into our minds when we think about God is the most important thing about us.
>
> The history of mankind will probably show that no people has ever risen above its religion, and man's spiritual history will positively demonstrate that no religion has ever been greater than its idea of God. Worship is pure or base as the worshiper entertains high or low thoughts of God.
>
> For this reason the gravest question before the Church is always God Himself, and the most portentous fact about any man is not what he at a given time may say or do, but what he in his deep heart conceives God to be like. We tend by a secret law of the soul to move toward our mental image of God. This is true not only of the individual Christian, but of the company of Christians that composes the Church. Always the most revealing thing about the Church is her idea of God, just as her most significant message is what she says about Him or leaves unsaid, for her silence is often more eloquent than her speech. She can never escape the self-disclosure of her witness concerning God.
>
> Were we able to extract from any man a complete answer to the question, "What comes into your mind when you think about God?" we might predict with certainty the spiritual future of that man. Were we able to know exactly what our most influential religious leaders think of God

today, we might be able with some precision to foretell where the Church will stand tomorrow.[1]

There really is no escaping this question. At one point or another you will have to answer it.

Most people spend a lifetime avoiding the question, though, just as the other disciples did, afraid to admit what they really believe about who Jesus is. They live lives of quiet mediocrity, continually dwindling the ebb and flow of their original passion amidst a sea of religious activity. Their lives pass like a haze, painfully lacking purpose and mission.

But for the ones who do answer, who dare to answer— oh, these are the wild ones, the ones who become virtually unstoppable. These live lives of purpose and passion. They experience an adventure with a gloriously unsearchable God. Their hearts and minds unlock to receive revelations of beauty and grace to which no experience of earthly conjuring could ever compare. Like Peter, they cross that line, and there really is no going back.

And just as Peter did, they receive a promise—a gift of identity and purpose that far exceeds their previous existence. They get a new name, an identity born out of the affection of a holy God, and they receive a promise of authority, ruling and prevailing in realms beyond our earthly borders.

ONLY GOD CAN DO IT

Jesus makes clear that the answer to this all-important question isn't one we can produce alone, telling Peter, "For flesh and blood has not revealed this to you, but

My Father who is in heaven" (Matt. 16:17). The saying is true: it takes God to know God. Just as Paul says, God is unsearchable and His ways past finding out (Rom. 11:33). If this is true, then even what we pursue—what we reach for and worship with adoring hearts—is only what He has chosen to reveal to us.

Our very existence on earth and in eternity is defined by our answer to this question "Who do you say that I am?" but we don't, on our own, have a clue who this Man is! We know bits and pieces. We know what we are supposed to say. But if we can't answer the question with our whole heart, then we aren't really answering it. The husband who spouts off "Yes, honey, you look fine" never won any Brownie points with his wife.

We have to look Jesus in the eye and answer this one question. We have to face the reality of our own lack of real, experiential knowledge of Jesus. And in humility and hunger, we have to open ourselves to receive what He wants to give us of Himself from His Holy Spirit.

WHEN IT STRUCK MY HEART

I remember when this reality struck my heart. I was serving under Mike Bickle at the time, and we were in the midst of hosting our annual Onething young adult conference when he said something to me that stopped me in my tracks.

Mike is the founder of a prayer ministry called the International House of Prayer Kansas City (IHOPKC), where I served on staff for nine years. The core of the ministry calls young adults to worship-based prayer and fasting and wholehearted devotion to Jesus. The ministry prays around the clock—twenty-four hours a day, seven days a week, three hundred sixty-five days a year. You can walk in the doors in the wee hours of any given morning and still find a couple hundred young people praying for our city, the church, the lost, and everything in between.

I had moved to IHOPKC only five years prior because I wanted to spend my life at the feet of Jesus in prayer and worship. I considered myself a radical disciple of Jesus and had learned to spend long hours in the Bible and in ministry to God and His people.

But even after all that, I wasn't prepared for what Mike said to me that day at the conference. Not at all.

We were backstage between sessions. Mike had already spent the previous seven conference sessions that week preaching solely about the God-Man, Jesus. Several months earlier we'd decided we were going to focus our entire teaching theme at our conference on Jesus—His character, His emotions, His attributes, and His desires— and now Mike was preparing for his final message.

In those moments between his penultimate and final preaching sessions, Mike turned to me and said, "You know, we have no idea who this Man is that we are talking about. We are all in for the shock of our lives when we see this glorious Man face-to-face."

I remember being stunned—even offended! How could Mike say that? We'd just spent hours listening to him and others talk about Jesus and only Jesus. Moreover, I fancied myself as someone not entirely illiterate in God's Word. Surely I knew who Jesus was—for goodness' sake, I was a preacher of the Bible! Of course I knew this Man of whom we speak so freely in our churches.

I kept looking at Mike in disbelief, even as he looked down at his notes to prepare for his next session, where he would continue to teach the twenty-five thousand young adults who had gathered together for the conference. Truthfully, I don't think Mike Bickle knew what he had just done to me with his hoarse voice and simple words. He still had the same goofy smile on his face that he always has after finishing up his teaching sessions, but this time the smile lingered as he prepared for his next session and marked up his notes at his break-neck pace.

Whether Mike knew it or not, the Holy Spirit used that moment to convict my heart of this truth: I did not know Jesus. Not *really*.

It dawned on me in that moment in a new way that no matter how many sermons I may have heard or even preached on the subject, Jesus is more than a subject. He is a real Person with a real personality, and it pained me to realize I barely knew Him. I knew a lot *about* Him, but if I was honest—if Jesus came to me in that moment, looked me in the eye, and asked me, "Who do you say that I am?"—my answer would entail a lot of stuttering and foot shuffling.

I knew I had a choice to make in that moment. I could either continue my life as I had been, like a good travel agent pointing others to a beautiful destination, or I could actually go somewhere myself in God.

I knew that this would be a journey that involved risk, as there were and are things about Jesus that aren't politically correct in our society. There are sides to Jesus that are extremely offensive to our Western mind-set. There are commands Jesus makes to His disciples that I wish I could ignore.

But the ache I felt in that moment, I will never forget. It trumped the list of potential cons presented by this pursuit. For the first time in my life I couldn't bear the thought that there were depths in Jesus I did not know. There was a treasure of beauty I had not yet seen, but I knew it was there, and I knew it was mine for the taking. I knew that in all my years of being a good "radical" Christian, I had actually only dipped my toes into the fringes of that vast ocean that is the knowledge of Christ.

THERE'S SO MUCH MORE

I think of what John said as he finished his gospel: "And there are also many other things which Jesus did, which if they were written in detail, I suppose that even the world itself would not contain the books that would be written" (John 21:25, NAS). There is so much more to be experienced and discovered in the personality of Jesus that all the books in the world cannot contain it! It makes me ache with holy jealousy.

If there is more available to us, if there is more to see and touch and experience, than why are we content with so little? It's as if we spend our lives dancing around the pool but never experience the ocean. C. S. Lewis put it this way in his famous sermon "The Weight of Glory":

> If we consider the unblushing promises of reward and the staggering nature of the rewards promised in the Gospels, it would seem that Our Lord finds our desires not too strong, but too weak. We are half-hearted creatures, fooling about with drink and sex and ambition when infinite joy is offered us, like an ignorant child who wants to go on making mud pies in a slum because he cannot imagine what is meant by the offer of a holiday at the sea. We are far too easily pleased.[2]

I don't know about you, but I don't want to live my life on the fringes of experience, just hearing good sermons, reading and writing good books, or tweeting inspirational verses. Those are all fine things, but they are not enough. They're not really *knowing* Him. I think if we dared to pursue the knowledge of Jesus as He is, not as we have made Him to be, we are in for the greatest, most exhilarating ride of our lives.

But the truth is that too often our culture has defined who Jesus is to us. He's the personal Jesus, the homeboy Jesus, the teacher Jesus, the role model Jesus, the therapist Jesus, or even Jesus Christ Superstar. Jesus is very likely the most popular, the most hated, the most referenced, the most admired, the most ridiculed, the most friendly, the most despised, and the most loved figure in all of human history.

If we are honest, even the church has created its own different versions of Jesus. We've pieced together versions of Jesus that best suit our current sense of lack, creating an image of Jesus that's based on our own need and not necessarily biblical truth. We have Savior Jesus, healer Jesus, meek and gentle Jesus, Republican Jesus, tolerant Jesus, social justice Jesus, and the list goes on.

But who is He, really?

Jesus is not a subjective personality. He's not a mold we can fashion to meet our needs. He's not a genie in a bottle we can rub to get our wish. He's a real Person who existed in perfection long before you or I were ever created, and we can't change Him. Who He was in the beginning, when He called for light to burst forth into the chaos and darkness, is who He remains now. Who He was when He destroyed 99 percent of the entire world population by sending a flood of destruction upon the entire planet is still who He is today. Who He was when He walked the earth in obscurity, humility, and meekness, demonstrating the glory of God in a human frame, is still who He is today. He has not changed.

He is a whole Person. He has thoughts and passions, anger and ache, and yet He is good, kind, and merciful. He is altogether more than we can imagine—more powerful, more vengeful, and more good.

And the truth is that we do not know Him. We have barely scratched the surface of the knowledge of this infinite, beautiful, holy Man. He is so much more than the leader of a religion or way of life. He's even so much more than our Savior, healer, or provider. The apostle

Paul made it crystal clear that Jesus is the center of all reality—that He is and will be preeminent in all things (Col. 1:18). Jesus possesses a majesty and a beauty that we can't even imagine. It's our great privilege to get to know this Person.

WHAT IS YOUR ULTIMATE DESIRE?

While imprisoned and waiting for his case to be heard before the emperor Nero, the apostle Paul wrote to the church in Philippi of his ultimate desire to "know [Jesus] and the power of His resurrection, and the fellowship of His sufferings, being conformed to His death" (Phil. 3:10). He made this statement after nearly thirty years of ministry spent facing some of the most difficult circumstances and having one of the most dramatic experiences with the risen Lord. Nonetheless, without hyperbole, Paul stated that his ultimate desire was to know Jesus more.

Paul's statement should devastate all our assumptions about what we know of Jesus and our own intimate friendship with Him. If Paul the Apostle, a man who had actually seen Jesus in a post-Resurrection appearance, who spent the strength of his life preaching the good news and pursuing a greater knowledge of God each and every day, stated near the end of his life that the one thing he desired above all else was simply to *know Jesus*, this should disrupt our current view of our life's purpose.

In this one statement Paul revealed to us the *why* behind all his endeavors. He was not motivated by duty, responsibility, or sacrifice. He was motivated by desire.

He'd been utterly ruined by the beauty of Jesus. One encounter sparked the fire in his heart. Years of study further fueled the obsession. And a lifetime of obedience and proclamation only fanned that fire of desire in his heart for more of God. He provides a testament of just how fascinated the human heart can become with Jesus the more our knowledge of Him grows.

How Do You Answer?

You may not be able to answer that singular question— "Who do you say that I am?"—with assurance in this present moment. But even the realization that you don't know is a witness of His grace working in your heart. Jesus wants to be known so badly by you that He's given you the divine grace you need to answer the question in truth. He has given you His very Spirit, sent to the earth to help you, to comfort you, to reveal the beauty of Jesus to you, and to remind you of His words. He's done all that so your heart can answer this question not out of robotic religiosity but out of true and sincere love, flowing out of an encounter with His very Spirit.

You don't have to know your answer to the question right now—but you should want to know. The question is an invitation to a journey. It's one you answer with one weak but faith-filled, grace-brimming response, and then you keep responding to it for the duration of your life.

You see, once you really cross that line, once you really experience the revelation of Christ, however small or simple it may seem at first, it ruins you. You cannot go back. It's the hook of all hooks, the cliff-hanger of all cliff-hangers. Jesus becomes your obsession.

And He was meant to be your obsession all along. This is what your heart was created for—to be fascinated, challenged, caught up in something bigger, more grand, and far more wonderful than anything the human heart could conjure on its own. His glory is for us to see, to know, and to experience. Our hearts were made to encounter Him in a pure, holy, and consuming way.

He is the glory of God, the revelation and nearness of a holy, transcendent God, and He is fully man. Drawing near to us even in our weakness, He reveals what God is like—not far, stoic, and always angry, but rather kind, relational, deeply personal, and involved with the affairs of men. Ours is a God who sees all things—every man's hearts and thoughts—and still loves with a love that's unwavering, steady, waiting, and orchestrating the culmination of all things to Himself.

Jesus is far more beautiful and far more majestic than any of us can even imagine. He is the pearl of great price, the treasure buried in the field, the hidden glory that is reserved for kings to search out. And our chief desire in life should be to set a course of a long obedience in the same direction, to search out the "unsearchable riches of Christ" (Eph. 3:8) and to make Him forever our magnificent obsession.

He wants to be known this way. Do you want to know Him?

REFLECTION QUESTIONS

Who is Jesus to you? How would you answer the question "Who do you say that I am?"

In what ways are you desiring to know Jesus more? What are some practical ways you can reorient your life to purse a greater knowledge of God?

— — — — — — — —

Father of Glory, I ask today that You would fill me with the spirit of wisdom and revelation in the knowledge of Your beautiful Son, Jesus. I pray that the eyes of my understanding would be enlightened to see Him and to know Him in a greater way. Give me a living understanding of His beauty and worth, that I would live my life in obedience to the revelation that He is the Christ, the Lord of all. Reveal who I am to You, and help me to know the hope of my calling as a son/daughter of God. Consume me with passion and grace to pursue You with my whole heart for all my days. Amen.

Chapter 2

A LIFE OF ONE THING

But one thing is needed, and Mary
has chosen that good part, which
will not be taken away from her.

—LUKE 10:42

W E ARE IN a crisis of distraction. Lack of connection and the expectation of instant gratification is a crippling reality in our present age. Our
generation has largely lost the treasure of stillness before
God. With the advent of the Internet and the relative
ease of so-called connectedness via social networking, we
find ourselves busier than ever but deeply unfilled. We
fill our time with superfluous activities and yet the ache
for purpose and meaning remain profoundly imbedded
in our human experience. Distraction. Multitasking.
One random moment leads mindlessly to the next. We
are entangled in an endless web of entertainment and

information constantly available at our fingertips. We all struggle with this. But might there be a different way? Could we have been meant to live life differently?

A Woman Worried and Distracted

The fame of Jesus had been spreading through the region. Tales of His wonders had reached Jerusalem, Judea, Samaria, and even Syria. Great multitudes had begun to follow Jesus everywhere. He was so magnetic, so joyful, and so irresistible that even hardened Galilean fisherman left their nets to follow Him. People abandoned their very livelihood and means of provision just to follow after this One who was so beautiful and captivating.

What's more, the crowds were so numerous that if Jesus was coming to your house, you had to be prepared to possibly lose your roof. People were so desperate for one word or one touch from this Man that they were willing to bore a hole through a roof of their neighbor's house—or even the house of a complete stranger—and drop a man through so he could get nearer to Jesus.

By all reasonable observations, Jesus had attained Hebrew rock star status.

And now he'd come to Bethany to visit His closest friends, Martha, Lazarus, and Mary.

Surely we can relate to Martha's frantic state of preparation to receive and serve the King of kings, the promised Messiah of Israel, in her own house. Can't you just see her—chopping the onions and kneading the bread, rushing between the kitchen and the sitting room, ordering the servants about, and refilling all the cups? You can almost smell it—the baba ghanoush almost ready, the chickpeas being pressed for hummus. Something magical was in the making.

But it wasn't happening in the kitchen.

In the living room Jesus was speaking. All the disciples were gathered around, crammed into the room with all those who had also tagged along. He was telling His stories, sharing His wisdom, with everyone hooked on His every word. Those words that formed galaxies and set planets spinning in motion? They were falling upon human ears and awakening human hearts. The eternal Word took voice in human frame, and those gathered in that room must have leaned in, soaking up every drop of perfect and authentic life that proceeded from His mouth.

Time stood still in that living room.

Martha is busy in the kitchen. She's wiping the sweat from her forehead, adjusting her dress and dusting the flour from her skirt. Then she lets go of a deep breath and lifts the tray of food, walking out of the chaos and heat of the kitchen into the stillness of the living room. Looking around at the wide-eyed company in her care, she wonders at their awe. She hands a plate down to a man, motioning for him to pass it around.

Then, out of the corner of her eye, she sees Mary. Her younger sister. Sitting in front, right at Jesus's feet—still, silent, listening in raptured wonderment.

"What is she doing? It's ridiculous," Martha thinks. "Doesn't she know how much work is to be done? Why isn't she helping? She's not a child anymore. She ought to be helping me serve the guests!"

Martha moves across the room and puts herself directly into Mary's line of sight, trying her best to motion to her sister without disturbing the meeting. Mary looks down for a moment, and then, as if adjusting her seat, turns a bit, removing Martha from her range of vision.

Martha is furious. Of all the immature, ridiculous things to do!

With a huff, Martha takes her tray and hurries back to the kitchen for drinks. "If Mary thinks I'm going to handle all this on my own, she has another thing coming," she fumes.

She picks up the pitcher and proceeds into the living room with a plan of action. Walking over to Jesus, she interrupts Him for a moment, offering to refill His cup.

Jesus smiles up at her and says, "Thank you," offering her His cup.

She seizes her opportunity. "Oh, you're welcome, Lord. But do you see I'm serving all these people? There's much left to do, and Mary's not doing anything to help. Please, will you tell her to come and help me right now?"

With that, Martha flashes Mary a triumphant glance—truly the look of an older sister in the know.

Jesus gazes at Martha, her cheeks flushed with stress and frustration, her breath quickened by exasperated anger. He senses her feelings of annoyance and envy, and He smiles for a moment—she's always been a no-nonsense, cut-to-the-chase type of woman. He loves her boldness and spunk. And He understands her frustration.

But something is happening here—in this moment, in her home—and it's more important than refilled cups, well-seasoned hummus, and playing the good hostess. God is here in her home. He's drawn near, alive, and beautiful, and He is speaking. She need not be jealous or bustle about with formality. This moment was for Martha too, if she would just take hold of it as Mary had.

"Martha, Martha," He begins, His voice brimming with affection and a smile curling on His lips. Every joyous memory of their history together, every spunky Martha-moment and all the ways He'd enjoyed her personality, spilled into the tone of His voice.

He wasn't responding harshly. There was no spitting of rebuke or yelling of her name. On the contrary, he was doing what He did every time we see Him repeat a name in Scripture: giving a correction in deep tenderness. Remember these? "Simon, Simon, Satan has asked to sift all of you as wheat. But I have prayed for you" (Luke 22:31–32, NIV). "Jerusalem, Jerusalem…how often I have longed to gather your children together, as a hen gathers her chicks under her wings, and you were not willing" (Luke 13:34, NIV). "Saul, Saul, why do you persecute Me?" (Acts 9:4, NIV). We see that same tenderness and emphasis here in Luke 10—Jesus responding with patience and grace even while giving a correction.

I love this particular attribute about Jesus more than I can express. His kindness is captivating. Because you see, as much as I like to think of myself as Mary in this story, most of the time in my life, if I'm honest, I can relate to Martha. And when He comes to correct me, I want Him to say my name twice.

Jesus, in perfect knowledge and perception of the situation and Martha's seemingly justified irritation, reveals a desire in His heart that is staggeringly beautiful and simple: "Martha, Martha, you are worried and troubled about many things. But one thing is needed, and Mary has chosen that good part, which will not be taken away from her" (vv. 41–42).

GOD IN OUR MIDST

The crux of this passage does not pit service against devotion. Yes, service is vital in the kingdom of God, and Jesus calls us to serve people. But Martha had become so troubled and distracted in her service that she'd lost perspective on the eternal significance of the moment. Her worries and stresses caused her to miss the presence of God.

And can't we relate? Many times in our lives, we become distracted too, bogged down by worries and anxieties that rob us of encounters with God. Those distractions aren't always big things, either. Most of the time they're the small things that build up over time so that distraction, a troubled spirit, and crankiness become our default mode. It gets to the point that when we sit down to encounter God through His Word, all we can think about is having to do this or that or needing to check e-mail, Twitter, or Facebook.

Have we grown so accustomed to being worried and troubled that we've lost the ability to be still and listen to God? Have we grown so attached to distractions, justifiable or not, that we've lost sight of the eternal significance of the present moment?

I can promise you this. None of us will stand before the judgment seat of Christ on the last day and say, "Man, I wish I had posted a few more tweets in my life," or "I wish I had commented on that kid's Facebook wall a little more." No one is going to tell Jesus they wish they had more time to play video games or shop online. Rather, the focus will be on the time we spent cultivating a relationship of loving, joyful intimacy with Him, encountering His presence and walking in grace-filled obedience to His Word.

You see, as much as these distractions in our lives steal our joy, producing only more stress and worry, they also rob us of real, vibrant, life-giving encounters with the presence of God. I don't know about you, but I don't want an existence of stressed-out, overtired, overworked worry and angst. I want a joyful awareness of His presence in my life. I want to perceive His words when He speaks to me. I want to listen and obey.

Think about it this way. If faith without active obedience is dead (James 2:26), and if faith only comes by hearing (Rom. 10:17), and hearing comes by His Word (Rom. 10:17), how can we live a life of true Christ-pleasing obedience without first living from a place of devoted, quiet listening?

Here is the crux of this story and the beautiful message that the life of Mary of Bethany reveals to us: God is not looking for many things. He's not looking for busy, productive doers. He desires and values just one thing. What is that one thing? The cultivation of a loving, attentive relationship with Jesus. A listening and beholding heart.

CONSIDER IT ANOTHER WAY

In Psalm 27 we can view this idea from the vantage point of another heart that longed for just one thing. King David was a man whose seasons of life have become legend for the passing generations—how he defeated an enemy giant with only a sling and stones, how he rose and fell from favor with kings, how his sins and triumphs on display for all to see help us glean wisdom for ourselves. Here is a man greatly revered by history in both the Christian and Jewish traditions.

But who was David at his core?

We find a unique window into the heart behind this great man of history, where he begins by singing of a peace and light found only in God even in the midst of war and trouble. Then he sings this phrase:

> One thing I have asked from the LORD, that I
>   shall seek:
> That I may dwell in the house of the LORD all
>   the days of my life,
> To behold the beauty of the LORD
> And to meditate in His temple.
>   —PSALM 27:4, NAS

Here we see that David's heart song, the motivating factor of his life, was to behold the beauty of God and spend all his days adoring Him. This is the same David whom God called "a man after My own heart" (Acts 13:22), and surely this song of David's heart captured God's attention and delight.

Perhaps what moved God's heart when he looked at David was the fact that David was looking back—that he was longing, reaching, and adoring. Perhaps we can learn through this that God is looking for more than mere vessels to carry out His decrees. Perhaps God desires to find hearts fascinated by His beauty, souls that long to meditate upon and behold Him. Perhaps what David and Mary knew—but Martha didn't understand—was that God is looking for true friends.

THE SEARCH OF HEAVEN

Today the eyes of the Lord search to and fro across the earth to strongly support the hearts that are loyal to Him. He's searching for hearts full of love and attentiveness like those of Mary of Bethany and David. When He said of Mary, "This one thing shall not be taken from her," He meant it.

And He means it for all those who follow in the footsteps of this young woman from Bethany. He will fight from heaven to defend the one whose heart is fully His. He will jealously guard that relationship with the jealousy of a bridegroom. He will defend you in the midst of your enemies. Though they may ridicule you and misunderstand you, He will vindicate your faith and devotion for all the world to see when He returns in glory to the earth.

Your choice to spend hours browsing blogs and websites, to live busy and distracted, to serve and bustle about in anxiety? Those choices will not benefit you in eternity. But the choice to stop, to listen and hear His Word, to spend hours in prayer, to build a history of loving relationship with Jesus? That choice—that one thing—will carry on with you forever. It will not be taken from you.

You won't take clothing or food or possessions with you into the next age, but your history in God will endure. The treasure of your intimacy with Jesus will last. That time spent building a history in God, a friendship with Jesus, a communion with the Holy Spirit will endure through the next age. It's what will allow us to look back on our lives on this battleground called Earth, where the devil raged against every choice for love we ever made and sought to steal our love and attention, and gives us the confidence to say, "I chose well. I loved God with all my mind, heart, soul, and strength."

You see, the choice to love God is reserved only for human beings. And the choice to love Him in the midst of adversity and distractions is reserved only for the years of our lives on Earth. But the fruit of our choice to love Him carries on in eternity. Therefore, the choice to love God, to build a real, loving relationship with Him, is truly the wisest thing you can do in your life. It's what He's longing for and searching for in all the earth.

Think of it like a frantic spotlight from heaven that's searching to and fro across the Earth, peering into the hearts of people roaming across all nations. God is looking down from above, over the balcony of heaven, to find anyone who will look back. He longs for real relationship with you. Not jargon or empty words or even duty-driven obedience. He wants love.

And love cannot be chosen for you. No one else can choose this one thing for you, just like no one else can answer for you the question, "Who do you say that I am?" when Jesus asks. This journey is your own. You cannot live in the shadow of another man's devotion. You cannot live in the memory of a time when you were once devoted. You must choose this one thing daily.

A QUESTION OF WORTH

Is Jesus worth this devotion from you? Is He worth time spent in prayer, talking with Him, listening to His Word?

This question has haunted me over the years. Ever since I first read the story of Mary of Bethany and her extravagant devotion for Jesus, I have asked myself, "How much is He really worth to me?" While I have struggled to answer this question, I have also discovered that true joy is found when Christ occupies all of my thoughts, emotions, and being. I am never more at peace than when I'm at His feet, refusing all those distractions.

But be warned. Although this language of sitting at His feet, being quiet, and listening sounds docile, simple, and peaceful, it's the single most violent struggle you will face in your life. The enemy will never stop warring for your attention and affections. Until your life on the earth ends or Jesus returns, you will have to make a choice.

You see, what others attributed to Mary as laziness or just a quieter, more introverted personality type was actually a fierce, uncanny boldness and strength. Mary knew she should have been helping Martha serve. She knew her duties and what was expected of her. But she made a bold choice, a choice that defied her family, her cultural norms, and even her own sense of duty and reputation. She was desirous enough, desperate enough, and fascinated enough by Jesus to discard all those pressures. And Jesus would never forget her choice.

BE PREPARED

You cannot choose this one thing on the run. You cannot add it as a supplement to a crowded lifestyle. You must adopt a radical new view of life carried out under the leadership of the Holy Spirit. It's a violent choice. And it's not easy in the culture in which we live. It takes a real measure of spiritual violence to resist the distractions—even the permissible distractions—of our culture. It will disrupt and even offend those around you, just as Martha was genuinely flabbergasted, annoyed, and disrupted by Mary's choice to sit at the feet of Jesus.

Paul agreed. In 1 Corinthians 4:9 he says, "[I] have been made a spectacle to the world, both to angels and to men." In other words, men and angels look at us and say, "What manner of life are you living?"

Are you a spectacle to angels and men? Do even the angels take a step back at your lifestyle and say, "What an unusual work of God is happening in that man's or woman's life"?

Your choice to pursue God wholeheartedly will be misunderstood. It will be deemed over the top. I know because I have been told to calm down so many times.

Even my sister, a Harvard graduate, got apprehended with this vision of "wasting" her life at the feet of Jesus when she quit her prestigious job and abandoned her reputation. Her choice was utterly misunderstood. She was told to calm down and not waste those crucial years of her career life. She endured disappointment from people she loved and respected, and she even lost some friendships. But to this day she has not regretted that choice. It set her on a course of abandoned, wholehearted pursuit of Jesus, and though different seasons bring different time constraints and responsibilities, that "one thing" remains the primary reach of her heart.

Of course, the goal in choosing to dedicate ourselves to wholehearted pursuit of Jesus is not meant to be overtly offensive. The goal is to give ourselves wholly to God. I just want to assure you that those who do this will disrupt the lives of those near them.

We are living in a culture where many of the brightest ones—even godly men and women among us—operate with a different mind-set than this "one thing" mind-set. They have a different daydream in their hearts than this. If they were honest, they would say, "The *last* thing that I want with all my heart is to gaze on the beauty of the Lord. I want an anointed ministry first. I want certain dynamics in my family second. I want certain dynamics in my economics third. I want a certain measure of honor and friendships fourth. I want health fifth. Oh, OK, Lord, You're sixth. Not bad!"

The daydream of their heart is not what David describes.

But when that desire to behold the beauty of the Lord consumes your heart, when it becomes the one thing you desire as David did, it resets your whole priority system and worldview.

CULTIVATE A BEHOLDING HEART

How do we cultivate listening and beholding hearts like this? If a heart that beholds God, that listens and responds to Him, is truly what God is looking for in the earth, how do we do attain that? Furthermore, what would it look like for a whole generation's thought life to be filled with heaven? What would it look like for our conversations to flow out of that place of beholding, our passions and priorities aligned with the Holy Spirit's leadership and agenda?

The way we behold Him like that on this side of eternity is by taking time to focus our attention on Him in diligent prayer and study of His Word. Accordingly, I've provided some resources for you in the appendix sections of this book to help you go deeper into such study. Appendix A includes recommended reading for deeper study related to each individual chapter of this book, and Appendix B provides an outline for approaching a responsible study of the Bible. I encourage you to read through these resources and try them out.

My desire for this chapter was to give you a *why* to fuel the *what*. We serve and adore an unimaginably beautiful and glorious God. His heart is bent toward us. He longs to share His secrets, His majesty, and His mystery with us—to fascinate us for eternity. His words offer the truest satisfaction for the ache of the human heart. We were made to behold and hear Him. When we miss this in the hustle of our busy lives, we miss so much of who we are and so much of who He is.

I challenge you, then, to take the words of Jesus seriously. When He said, "One thing is needed," He wasn't kidding. Choose this simple way. Choose it daily. Fight to choose it above all else. And watch Him vindicate Your choice with His presence and power, time after time.

REFLECTION QUESTIONS

When you examine your life, what evidence do you find that your relationship with Jesus is the one thing that matters above all else?

What distractions hinder you from making your friendship with Jesus the priority in your life, particularly as it relates to your time, your resources, and your energy?

— — — — — — — — —

Father, I pray that You would fascinate my heart with Your beauty. I want to behold Your Son and be consumed with passion for Him. Though I know my heart is prone to wander and to distraction, lead me into deeper friendship with Your Son. Help me to turn my eyes from worthless things and to fix my eyes on the author and finisher of my faith. Lord, I want to be a person of one thing. I want this to be my primary ambition, my consuming thought. As King David did, I cry out to You: one thing I ask, this will I seek, that I may behold You in Your beauty and meditate on Your glorious splendor all the days of my life. Amen.

Chapter 3

THE GOD WHO RESPONDS

Jesus wept.

—JOHN 11:35

HAVE YOU EVER felt an ache you just don't have language for? That feeling of a deep, often secret and indescribable dissatisfaction with life? I believe this sense of longing—which every human feels—are whispers of Eden. We're born remembering it. In the depths of our souls, whether we have language to express it or not, each of us longs for God. We were created to walk with Him in the cool of the day as we bear His image.

And no matter how far we fall, no matter how many generations pass, we human beings cannot escape the sense that we were made for more than this current fallen state. It's what I call the "God-shaped hole" inside us, and it's why we're so dissatisfied with life. It's why we crave more, bigger, better, faster, stronger. It's why no matter how far up the ladder we climb, we still lay our heads on our pillows at night feeling lost, sad, and utterly unfulfilled.

But it wasn't meant to be so. Real, vibrant relationship with Jesus is your portion in this life and in the ages to come. The reason He made you to have that ache, that "God-shaped hole," is because He intends to satisfy you with His love. And I'm not talking about some emotional, ethereal concept of love here, either. I'm talking about relationship. I'm talking about a partnership with His ways and in His kingdom, about dominion and authority in the place of prayer, living in an abiding, leaning, growing, vibrant, everyday relationship.

We weren't meant to lurch through a shadow life of ache and disappointments, of endless wanderings and dissatisfaction. No, real joy and an experience of fellowship were meant for us. From the very beginning when God thought of the human race, He designed us for deep interaction with Him. And it's an interaction that goes both ways. We were made to receive His love for us.

Do you want to know how I know? Let's turn again to the life of Mary of Bethany.

THE GOD WHO WEEPS

We know her now as the one who chose the one thing needed, the one who refused distractions and esteemed Jesus as worthy of her time and attention even at the risk of her own sister's public rebuke. But the next stage in Mary of Bethany's journey is even more profound, giving us a glimpse into Jesus's heart and response toward those who love Him that way.

This next episode of Mary's journey is found in John 11. Jesus and His disciples are outside Bethany, about a half day's journey away. He has continued to preach and perform miracles where He goes, and crowds continue to follow Him. But a large amount of controversy circles Him now as well. Tension has risen, and many of the religious leaders resent His fame and power. The starstruck stupor of the people has begun to wear off. If Jesus really was the political Messiah they'd been waiting for, why hadn't He risen to greater power to overthrow the Roman occupation? He walks in favor with God—that much is clear. How else could He perform such signs and have such wisdom? Even so, what is He waiting for?

But Jesus just doesn't fit the mold of expectation. A sense of unrest is rising in the people, a clear dividing line—either you love Him or you hate Him.

Then word comes to Jesus that Lazarus, His dear friend, is sick and on the verge of death. The disciples are concerned. They know how Jesus loves Lazarus and his sisters, Mary and Martha.

"Jesus, let's go to Lazarus right now," they say. "You heard that he is sick. Surely there's something You can do."

But Jesus surprises them and says no. "It is not yet time. This will not end in death and sorrow but will end in the glory of God."

I'll pause right here and say that Jesus is the best storyteller that ever lived. He's setting up the tension that

He is going to resolve. He knows better than anyone that Lazarus is about to die, but He's going to reveal Himself as the resurrection, the truth, and the life, so He lets certain things unfold that the natural human mind can't fully comprehend. When all is said and done, this story is going to bring the greatest amount of glory and pleasure to the Father as Jesus reveals Himself to be more than a mere man, more than a prophet or teacher, and more than a political answer to an oppressed nation.

Well, we know what happens. Lazarus does, in fact, die. Word comes to Jesus, and He begins His journey to Bethany. He certainly doesn't rush along, though, because we know by the time He gets there, Lazarus has been dead and entombed for four days (v. 39).

While Jesus is still on the outskirts of the city, Martha hears of His arrival and runs out to Him. Weeping, she cries, "Lord, if You had been here, my brother would not have died. But even now I know that whatever You ask of God, God will give You" (vv. 21–22).

Jesus assures her that her brother will rise again, and Martha replies, "I know that he will rise again in the resurrection at the last day" (v. 24).

Then Jesus looks at Martha with deep compassion— and surely a twinkle in His eye. He knows her suffering and grief, and He knows the hope and comfort He will give her if she'll receive it. He says, "I am the resurrection and the life; he who believes in Me will live even if he dies, and everyone who lives and believes in Me will never die. Do you believe this?" (vv. 25–26, NAS).

What a statement! He just puts it plainly. The hope of Israel—well, far beyond that to the hope of all humanity, who since the fall of Adam have lived under the penalty of sin, which is death—is found in Christ. Jesus pronounces hope. And Martha responds well, saying, "Yes, Lord; I have believed that You are the Christ, the Son of God, even He who comes into the world" (v. 27, NAS).

This is such a profound moment in history—Jesus's declaration of who He is, Martha's statement of faith, plus the wonders that follow—but something even more profound, at least in my opinion, is about to happen here. Something precious is hidden in these verses that reveals a facet of God's heart toward us.

After Martha's interaction with Jesus, she goes to Mary and tells her, "The Teacher is here and is calling for you" (v. 28, NAS). This verse says she does this *secretly.* Why? Maybe Martha is admitting her level of relationship with Jesus pales in comparison to Mary's. Maybe she remembers Mary had touched something in God's heart when she first was found sitting and listening to Jesus's words. Maybe she thought Mary would evoke something different in Jesus, that He would respond differently to her. Whatever her reasons, Martha keeps it secret.

But as soon as Mary hears Jesus is there, she gets up and runs to where Jesus is and throws herself at His feet. (Interestingly, all three times you see Mary in Scripture, she's at the feet of Jesus, revealing her humility, her teachable spirit, and her heart of worship.) She throws herself at the feet of Jesus and says with a broken heart,

"Lord, if You had been here, my brother would not have died" (v. 32).

Well, when Jesus saw Mary weeping, He groaned in the Spirit and was troubled. And then we see it—the shortest verse in Scripture, but perhaps one of the most powerful. John 11:35 tells us, "Jesus wept." The eternal God-Man, the Man who knew no sin, the God who created the universe with His Father, looks upon a young woman weeping for her brother and *He weeps*.

OUR RELATIONAL GOD

What's more amazing—the Man who can raise the dead or the God who can weep with His friends? When I read this portion of Scripture, I always ask myself this question. Somehow our minds have intellectualized God to the point that we have made Him this distant, stoic, unemotional, uninvolved God in the affairs of humanity, like somehow He created the earth like clockwork and set it into motion and then said, "OK, now run."

As Christians, while we know that isn't true, we live with a practical atheism. Our minds know in theory God is good, kind, and attentive, but we live our daily lives as if He isn't. Our default mode is to assume God doesn't see us or care about us. Therefore, when we approach God, we don't come to Him as though He is a tender, merciful God who has deep emotions in response to encountering His friends. One of the clearest messages Jesus brought to humanity is that God desires to draw near to us because He deeply loves us, yet it is the message most difficult to grasp on the heart level.

Take a moment and ponder this. Why do you really think Jesus came to earth? Or go back even further. Why did God create man at all? We know the verse by heart: "For God so loved the world..." (John 3:16). We know what to say and how to sound Christian. We know that God is love.

But we approach that verse with a thousand presuppositions about love. We come with the fantastical Hollywood perception of love in mind or a perception of love based on our own experience, whether from a parent, a friend, or a spouse. Each person has their own idea and experience of love, so when we think of God and envision Him as a God of love, we have our own idea of what that means.

But one thing universally understood about love is that it is relational. It cannot exist alone, directed at nothing. Love seeks to give out, to grow, and to thrive. Love is ever moving, extending itself to the object of its affection, whether reciprocated or not. This is the nature of God and His kingdom rule.

Do you realize what this means? God is, in His nature, a *relational* God. Personable. Reaching. Feeling. Longing. Love flows out of Him and is sourced from Him. Love isn't something He does or puts on. It's His very nature. He's a God with a burning heart. Everything He is and does emanates love, a desire to relate and engage with you.

The proof of God's commitment and flow of relationship is the very fact of the Trinity. In eternity past the Trinity dwelt together in a deeply satisfying fellowship, and the most amazing thing is that this satisfied, pleasing fellowship, this deeply mutual and open-hearted interaction, is what we are invited to participate in. Our God created us for deep, loving relationship. It is the original intent of mankind, created in His likeness, to commune in fellowship with the Godhead.

This is the lens from which we should read, study, memorize, and meditate. This is the truth from which we should live and orchestrate our lives. To be partakers of this divine communion—this is what your heart aches for in the very depths. This is what fills that "God-shaped hole" within you. Fellowship with God. Relationship with a God of burning, holy love. He burns for you, and you were made to burn for Him.

His Commitment to You

This is who Jesus is. This is the story He's writing. We are not just nondescript servants and workers in a vast crowd. We have a dynamic part in the story of His glory! It's the reason He gave everything to redeem us. This holy, glorious relationship was too wonderful for Him to give up. When the angels fell, He did not go after them. But when humanity fell, oh, He paid the greatest price to go after us and bring us back. This is His love for you.

This is truly one of the most life-changing revelations, and it's a shame because so many of us don't know it. God's love, in many senses, is Christianity 101, but we have gotten so far from Christianity 101. We are caught in our web of sin. We are caught in our cycles of shame and unbelief, and we have no real confidence in the blood of Jesus to make us clean and whole.

His plan for your life doesn't stop with a prayer of salvation. From the beginning of time He purposed for Himself a people redeemed from all nations and tribes to love and delight in and to rule His kingdom in partnership with Him. It's the reason He gave everything to redeem us.

It's outrageous, but we don't fully comprehend that the God we serve is *for us*. Every time we say yes to Him, His heart is toward us. He doesn't withhold Himself. He doesn't give us the cold shoulder because we're immature. He's not a God who is far off, unconcerned, or upset with us. He's not a God who is waiting for us to get our act together. He is near us even now— not only in a memory of nearness reserved to history as a Man who once walked the earth, but rather as a Good Shepherd who stays near, watching, overseeing, loving, and tenderly leading in this present moment in our daily lives. He's fully involved, fully relational, and fully committed to finish the good work He began in us, not because He has to but because He wants to.

He is more committed to you than you can ever imagine. His heart desires you more than you know. But you must open your heart. You must let God love you. Let Him enjoy you in your weakness. Let Him heal you and prove He is safe and tender. Let Him show you what true, pure, and life-giving love really is.

This passage in Song of Solomon captures the longing in God's heart for us to let Him love us:

Let Me see your face,
Let me hear your voice;
For your voice is sweet,
And your face is lovely.

—SONG OF SOLOMON 2:14

God longs for us to behold His glory in the secret place, not only because He deserves our attention, but also because He actually wants our love! An exchange of love happens between us and Him. Our love moves God's heart. Our love impacts Him. Our love delights Him and makes Him happy. We behold God because it moves our hearts, because it awakens and revives us, but it stirs and affects Him as well.

THE GOD WHO DELIGHTS IN YOU

You have ravished my heart,
My sister, my spouse;
You have ravished my heart
With one look of your eyes,
With one link of your necklace.

—SONG OF SOLOMON 4:9

In this Song of Solomon passage we find a metaphor for how God speaks to His bride, the church. God is saying here, "With just one look, with just one movement of your heart toward Me, I am undone. I am ravished!"

Can you believe what this means? It's staggering to comprehend, but somehow even our weakest glance moves God. God is looking across the earth, searching hearts and minds to find even one person looking up at Him, saying,

"Jesus, I love you." And when He finds the gaze of His beloved one, something erupts in the heart of God.

That is what John 11 shows us—that our God is a God of deep emotions and deep passion for us and that He knows how to empathize with us. Like He wept with Mary, He is intimately aware of and emotionally present with you today.

When you come into contact with this truth, I promise it will change the way you think about and approach God. This revelation will invigorate your heart and give you the sustaining grace you need for this journey of faith. And I can say this because I've experienced it to be true for myself.

One day when working out a disagreement with my wife, Grace, I remember she threw her hands up and asked me, "What do you really want, Brian?"

I paused and then answered, "Honestly, at the end of the day I just want to make Him smile."

I remember thinking it was a pretty good answer at the time. It ended our conversation on a high note. I felt like I had won theologically. All was well.

Well, a few weeks passed and that incident was completely forgotten. Then one morning I was driving to work and felt the gentle tug of the Holy Spirit on my heart. I heard Him say, "Brian, you know a few weeks back when you told Grace all you really wanted was to make Me smile?"

"Yes, I remember," I replied. "That was pretty good, huh?"

"Brian," He said, "you always have My smile."

Tears filled my eyes in that moment, and I began to gently weep, right there in my car, just driving to work, as the Holy Spirit did what He does best—pour the love of God into my heart and direct me into truth.

You see, I am Korean-American, and I was raised in a pretty typical Korean home—Christian and loving, but pretty stereotypical in its emphasis on perfect grades, respect toward elders, and high expectations for success. As I've grown older, I've continued to realize how much my upbringing shaped my view of God and how I perceived He felt about me. I was always a very driven and decisive person, but in that moment in the car, as I felt the Holy Spirit's presence, I realized my motivation was to prove myself to a God who was already completely delighted in me.

Of course, I knew in theory He loved me and accepted me. I had all the language for it. But the Lord isn't content with our lofty verbiage. He's committed to revealing His love to us, to peeling back layer after layer of our unbelief and wrong mind-set until we really believe the truth and love Him in return.

That's what I learned that day. And that's what God wants for you too.

To encounter this fiery, eternal love of God, to grasp His intention for your life as one of real, vibrant relationship, is to receive the greatest level of grace for perseverance in this pilgrimage of faith. It's like a father opening his arms to his child who is learning to walk. With a big smile and encouraging words, He invites the child to come into the embrace.

The Father's smile, the Bridegroom's passion, and the Spirit's grace is your fuel in this journey. You will fall a thousand times, but what will quicken your heart to rise again? The delight and desire of God. This is the joy set before us: to respond to His furious, blazing, outrageous invitation of love.

WHAT COULD HAPPEN?

If you dared to believe in this love He offers you, you would become unstoppable. If you dared to believe God delights in you—even in the toddling-along, learning-to-walk stages—what would you fear? Probably nothing. A real encounter and continued faith in the outrageous, unending, unconditional love of God radically changes your perspective. You begin to see His judgments are the kindness and care of a Father. His wrath becomes the burning zeal of a jealous Bridegroom. His rebuke becomes the wise pruning of His Holy Spirit. Sin becomes disgusting. Fear of man? What can man do to you? What do man's opinions matter in light of your eternal Father's?

You begin to live a life rooted in and directed toward eternity. The things of earth grow strangely dim, the trials of life suddenly make sense, pregnant with purpose and opportunity for eternal reward, and our Christian walk becomes a vibrant, burning, and shining relationship with our Savior on this side of time. Your life begins to scream transcendence. Others begin to notice a change in you, and they're provoked to run deeper into God too because of the evidence of His love and intimate friendship in your life. You live holy. And miracles spring forth from this place.

Remember Mary, weeping at Jesus's feet? Her confidence in His goodness hadn't changed. Her expectation of His power remained intact. It was the exchange of love from her heart to His that moved Him, and He responded with the greatest miracle He had performed up to that point: raising Lazarus from the dead. Islam's Allah never did that for anybody. Buddha never did that for a single person. But our God is an awesome God who is near the broken-hearted.

Even in the midst of your weakness and your brokenness, He has deep emotions for you. He weeps with those who weep. He rejoices with those who rejoice. Why? Because He is the best friend you could ever have, and that is what friends do.

Circling back to that question I asked earlier, I want to know and worship the Man who can raise the dead, and I want to worship the God who can weep with His friends. I want to know them both, because it is one Man. It is the God-Man. This is the Man who has the power to raise the dead and, at the same time, is the uncreated God who weeps and has deep emotions for His friends.

He feels, He desires, and He longs for real, deep relationship with you. It's why He made you like Himself. It's why He carved out a longing in your heart that only He can satisfy. He wants you to know His love because it will ruin you, it will fulfill you, and it will awaken your heart from the sin-and-shame-induced slumber you have endured your entire life.

But most of all, when you experience His love, you will love Him. And He longs for your love.

REFLECTION QUESTIONS

How would you describe God's emotions toward you?

What thought patterns cause you to have low opinions of who you are to God? How can you take captive those thoughts and fill your mind with what the Scriptures reveal about how God really feels about you?

Is there someone in your life that you can encourage today in how God feels about them? Ask the Holy Spirit to direct you to one person to encourage in the love of God today.

— — — — — — — — —

Father, today I ask that You would grant me, according to the riches of Your glory, to be strengthened with might through Your Spirit in my inner man. I pray that Christ may dwell in my heart and that I would be rooted and grounded in Your love. I ask You to enable me to comprehend with all the saints what is the width, length, depth, and height of Your love. Lord, I believe— help my unbelief! I long to know the love of Christ, though it surpasses knowledge. I want to comprehend Your emotions of love and delight in me. I want to know and believe that You see me, You know me, and You love me, even in my weakness. Awaken my heart to love You in return. Amen.

Chapter 4

AN EXTRAVAGANT DEVOTION

Assuredly, I say to you, wherever this gospel is preached in the whole world, what this woman has done will also be told as a memorial to her.

—Mark 14:9

WHAT IS A memorial? The qualifications of a memorial usually include extraordinary acts of heroism in humanity. Thinking of people such as Martin Luther King Jr., Abraham Lincoln, or Mother Teresa. A memorial is something we build to celebrate or commemorate monumental accomplishments of humanity, military victories, and even to soberly remember and learn from horrific atrocities throughout history (such as the Holocaust Museum, 9/11 Memorial, World War II memorials). Men commemorate feats of greatness. We build memorials to remember, to glean wisdom and insight from the past, and to honor and esteem the brightest of our generations. But what does God remember?

When we consider Jesus's statement in Mark 14:9, we see a staggering insight in to what God esteems. He literally says of a human being, their story is worth remembering forever. What is it about Mary of Bethany that so moved the heart of Jesus? He mandated that wherever His story is told in the whole world, hers would be also.

MARY OF BETHANY'S THIRD EXAMPLE

If Luke 10 is the outer courts and John 11 is the inner courts, Mark 14 is the holy of holies in the story of Mary of Bethany. It is the crux of what her life teaches us and the implications for those of us who desire to live abandoned and completely wholehearted toward Jesus.

Leading up to this passage is actually the beginnings of crisis in Jesus's life, when the Pharisees and the Sadducees are conspiring together on how they might kill Him. Then, immediately following this passage, in Mark 14:10 we see Judas Iscariot begin to betray Jesus. So bookmarked between the two major crises of the life of our Savior, we find this beautiful story of Mary of Bethany nestled right in the tension:

> And being in Bethany at the house of Simon
> the leper, as He sat at the table, a woman came
> having an alabaster flask of very costly oil of
> spikenard. Then she broke the flask and poured
> it on His head. But there were some who were

indignant among themselves, and said, "Why was this fragrant oil wasted? For it might have been sold for more than three hundred denarii and given to the poor." And they criticized her sharply.

But Jesus said, "Let her alone. Why do you trouble her? She has done a good work for Me. For you have the poor with you always, and whenever you wish you may do them good; but Me you do not have always. She has done what she could. She has come beforehand to anoint My body for burial. Assuredly, I say to you, wherever this gospel is preached in the whole world, what this woman has done will also be told as a memorial to her."

—Mark 14:3–9

Mary of Bethany was likely an orphan child along with her sister, Martha, and brother, Lazarus, as the Scriptures make no reference to their parents and where they lived was called "Martha's house." It seems most likely that when their parents died, they gave Martha the house as her inheritance and Mary this alabaster flask of very costly oil. Matthew tells us the alabaster flask was worth about a year's wages. Comparing that to today's economy, that would mean it was worth anywhere from thirty thousand to seventy thousand dollars.

Now, Mary was the only one of all of Jesus's disciples, even John the Beloved, who recognized what Jesus was going through. She'd been listening and had noticed the alarms and references Jesus kept making to His coming death. Somehow she was the only one who understood.

Because she was sitting at His feet continually, listening to His words, she recognized what He was about to do at the Passover. She remembered what John the Baptist said about Jesus: "Behold! The Lamb of God who takes away the sin of the world!" (John 1:29). She took Jesus's words seriously when He said, "I am going to go away. I am going to die, but in three days I will be raised from the dead, and I will be with you again." (See John 2:19; 16:7.)

The disciples had no understanding of what Jesus was saying because their vision of the Messiah was that of a conquering Messiah—one who wouldn't come in lowliness and obscurity. They were still waiting for His day of glory, so to speak, when He would stand and reveal Himself as the Messiah and live up to the prophecies of what the Messiah would do: free the Jewish people from oppression and establish Israel as the glory of the whole earth.

But Mary beheld Jesus, and she heard His words. Somehow, while everyone else filtered Jesus's words and lessons through the lens of their own ambitions and expectations, Mary just listened to what He was saying, and believed. She took His words seriously and pondered them in her heart. "He is about to suffer and die," she thought. "He is about to give everything. Oh, what can I do for Him?" Her heart longed to respond to what she perceived as His immeasurable worth.

You can almost imagine Mary contemplating what to do: "What do I have that I could give the King of kings and the Lord of lords who is everything?" I imagine her mind quickly flew to this alabaster flask of costly oil that represented her past, her present, and her future—her past because it was the only thing that linked her to her father and mother; her present, as it was the most valuable thing she had; and her future because it was likely meant to be a dowry to her future husband, that she might have financial and physical security in the days to come. Mary of Bethany looked at this alabaster flask, knowing it would mean giving everything and keeping nothing back for herself—no financial security in the future, only the ability to trust God completely—and she gave it anyway.

I can imagine she was crying as she came through the door with that flask of alabaster oil, the only one who knew what she was about to do. She removed the top from the flask—actually, it says in another part of Scripture that she broke the flask (Mark 14:3), meaning she wasn't just going to pour a little bit of the oil on Jesus; she was going to use it all, and she'd never get it back—and poured it over Jesus's head.

You can imagine all the disciples just chatting away, enjoying the meal and conversation, when suddenly the fragrance of this extravagant sacrifice began to permeate the room. Everybody stopped. Everybody stared. And for a moment, everybody wondered: "What in the world did Mary just do?"

Then the people sitting in the room began to berate Mary. It says they began to criticize her sharply. You can just hear them: "Mary, you crazy woman! What are you doing? That is worth a year's wages. You could have sold that and given it to the poor. Why this waste?"

I promise you this. A heart that shows radical passion and devotion for Jesus will rock the status quo every single time, and when that status quo is rocked, even the most religious among us will begin to criticize sharply. Why? Because in our core, we know this is the logical response of a heart that's been redeemed by the precious blood of Jesus. Radical, sacrificial love exposes the barrenness of our own choice to give "just enough," to love "within reason," and to live in a way that's practically no different than unbelievers.

I mean, think about it for a moment. The ones who sharply criticized Mary were the same ones who'd been with Jesus since the start of His ministry. They'd heard His sermons, seen the miracles He performed, and had, by all reasonable accounts, given up everything to follow Him. They were the radicals of their generation. In fact, just fifty days later at Pentecost these were the ones who were going to be empowered by the Holy Spirit to become the super-apostles of their day. These guys became the revivalists, the revolutionaries, and the faith-filled, but they looked at Mary on that day, seeing the broken jar of costly perfume, her tears, and the way she was giving everything to Jesus, and they rebuked her.

What happened in the heart of God when Mary broke the alabaster flask? What was Jesus's response? He said, "Leave her alone!"

His tone stunned them all for a moment. There was passion in His voice, a ferocity that shook them from their criticism. He rose to her defense, strong on her behalf.

"She has done a good thing for me," He said. "She has done what she could. She has prepared my body beforehand for burial."

Can you just imagine this for a moment? This alabaster flask was not filled with the cheap perfume we have today. It was filled with the very costly oil of spikenard, likely imported from India. Its scent is thick and intensely strong. It wasn't meant to be poured out in excess—one drop was enough. But this oil was poured out upon Jesus, flowing down onto His garments and soaking into His beard, hair, and skin. One week later when Jesus would be whipped, bloodied, and beaten, stripped naked and utterly alone, the fragrance of this oil would remain with Him. While Jesus was walking that road to Golgotha with the cross upon His back, completely stripped, naked, and scorned, one thing would comfort His heart: that fragrance of extravagant devotion.

And can you imagine Mary of Bethany? She then carried the aroma of this costly oil as well. Its heavy scent permeated her skin and hair too. I wonder if anyone noticed that Mary, one of the few who went to Jesus at the cross, carried the same fragrance He did.

You've experienced for yourself the way our sense of smell triggers something unique in our memory. It is the one thing that lasts longest with us. More than what we see, more than what we listen to, it's said the sense of smell stays with us the longest and triggers the most intense and vivid memories.[1] This is what Jesus takes to the cross—the smell of spikenard. Mary's privilege was bringing comfort to the heart of Jesus as He endured the greatest suffering any man has ever known.

A PROPORTIONATE RESPONSE

But what kind of privilege will we have if we give our lives to Jesus completely, if we follow the Lamb wherever He goes? Can you imagine how His heart is moved at our devotion?

I work with young people every day who long to make an impact in their generation. I talk with young and old alike who crave purpose and seek to make a mark on the world. But here is the key to making an impact in the earth: *give yourself wholeheartedly to God.* I don't mean throwing your hands up in a worship service. I mean *give yourself wholeheartedly to God.* Devote your life to the radical, unbalanced, extravagant pursuit of God. Follow Him in obedience to His Word, prayer, fasting, giving, holiness, and devoting your life to fulfill His commandments and the Great Commission. In the midst of a wicked and perverse generation, while nations rage and peoples plot against the Lord, make it your aim to be a pleasing aroma to God's heart, just as Mary was. Then when God looks down from heaven, when He leans in to hear the cries of men, His heart will be comforted by your love in the midst of all the accusation and rage brought against Him from all corners.

A life of devotion pleases God. And rather than making it your aim to be remembered in history, make it your aim to be remembered by heaven's account—just as Mary of Bethany is, whose story of extravagant, sacrificial love is told wherever the gospel is preached, even to the ends of the earth, so that all nations and peoples would know and understand. This is what God is looking for. This is the right response to the good news of Jesus.

Extravagant love for God is the right response to the cross. People will always be looking for a way to stay near the fence. They'll tell you to calm down, to not live so radically. They will tell you you're doing OK when you aren't. They'll constantly push you toward more "balance."

We don't need more balance when it comes to obedience to God. We need burning men and women who are completely ruined in love for God. What did Jesus tell that rich young man? "Sell all of your possessions, give to the poor, and follow after Me." (See Matthew 19:21; Mark 10:21; Luke 18:22.) These are radical demands, but when you realize who Jesus is, it is worth it to pour out your life at His feet.

You should expect to be misunderstood. Your life should provoke a response in others. "Why this waste?" they'll ask. It's an accusation that will afflict every heart that sets itself on this journey. But I love the way Nate Saint, a missionary and fellow martyr with Jim Elliot in South America, answered this accusation when it confronted him: "People who do not know the Lord ask why in the world we waste our lives as missionaries. They forget that they too are expending their lives...and when the bubble has burst, they will have nothing of eternal significance to show for the years they have wasted."[2]

You see, we're all wasting our lives on something. You're going to give your life in passion to *something*. What is that something for you?

God will confront every single idol of our hearts. He is more precious than our possessions. He is more precious than the people around us. He is more precious than all of our plans. Jesus is worth following. He is worth breaking the alabaster box of your lives over. He is worth the devotion and love of every human heart for all generations. He is worthy of ceaseless worship and adoration. And He is worthy of your love.

You have one life—one chance to love extravagantly, one chance to choose Him in the face of a thousand distractions and a thousand accusations. This is the gift you have to give. This is your alabaster jar. You're going to waste your life on something. What will it be? How much is He worth to you?

You see, taking up your cross to follow Him, abandoning all lesser things, refusing the so-called comforts of this world, choosing the good part, and pouring out your life in love for Him, this is your gift. This is your love. It isn't sacrifice when it's love. It is costly, yes. But "if a man would give for love all the wealth of his house, it would be utterly despised" (Song of Sol. 8:7). He would be utterly despised by the onlookers who deem his actions the ultimate foolishness, but the onlookers would be utterly despised by that man as well—what in all the world is more precious than love? It is foolish to the world.

Will you be misunderstood? Yes. Will you be mocked and scorned? Yes. Will you endure persecution? Yes. The Bible promises these things. But where else could you go? A ruined heart has no alternative. Real love burns every bridge. Real love risks playing the fool. Real love doesn't look back.

I remember thinking when I first fell in love with my wife, "It's her or no one." People laughed at that sentiment. But I absolutely meant it, and to this day I truly believe I would never have gotten married if Grace hadn't said yes. It was her or no one. And I risked everything for her yes. I was foolish and clumsy while doing it, and it cost me everything—I literally went broke pursuing her!—but I have never regretted it.

Love isn't a tithe. Love never chooses the bare minimum. Jesus didn't tithe Himself to the winning of mankind in love forever. He didn't give just the necessary measure. He gave everything He could possibly give. And this is the example He set for every believer and follower to come. This is love: that seemingly foolish Man hanging nailed to a crossbeam, bloody and barely recognizable, giving His life because love compelled Him. Unwilling to let you perish in your sin, He paid it all. He abandoned all semblance of self-preservation. He held nothing back.

This is the pathway into fellowship with Jesus. This is the way into true life—laying down our lives, loosening our grip on self-preservation and self-love, and picking up a cross instead.

Most people want to stay safe, comfortable and non-disruptive. But love is not safe or comfortable. Love does not cling to the fence. Love races to the prize.

It Costs Everything

Too often we forget that following Jesus means that our journey will take us through Calvary. To be Christian is to be like Christ, even in the likeness of His death on a cross. And despite His challenge to take up our cross daily and follow after Him (Luke 9:23), we hesitate. We wonder, "Does He really mean that? Is this really what He requires?"

For those of us who live in a Western context, most of the time we dismiss this verse altogether. Because what is our context for a cross? What is our context for suffering and enduring hardship? We don't even have a grid for it, and we frequently dismiss this part of Scripture as something relevant to Christians in another part of the world—those enduring persecution or living in poverty. In fact, don't we do that with almost all the "suffering" verses? In the Western church persecution is almost a completely foreign concept, yet the Scriptures are clear that trials and persecutions should be expected by believers—*all* believers (John 16:33).

Following Jesus is more than a conversion prayer. It's a journey of walking how He walked. But the way is narrow. The path is difficult. Easy believism is not the way to God, and it is certainly not the way to a thriving, vibrant heart or a life that makes impact on the earth.

When you think of heroes of the faith or read amazing missionary stories, what do you feel? Inspired? Provoked? Excited? These are supposed to be normal stories. They are supposed to be commonplace in Christianity today. Their testimonies are supposed to be ours—stories of daring faith and fervent prayers answered with miracles, salvation, demons fleeing, prison doors opening, and blind eyes coming to see.

We should not settle for cheap or plastic religion. We should not settle for lofty verbiage or rhetoric that isn't real in our day to day. I want real Christianity. Don't you? I long for this generation to know apostolic Christianity, the kind of faith and fervor the early Christians walked in.

In case you don't know exactly what that looks like, there's an entire book of the Bible that will enlighten you. It's called the Book of Acts. You'll read how the early church fasted for days, gathered in prayer, was mighty in the Scripture, shared all things in common, spoke with boldness, turned cities upside down, saw healings and miracles, laid hands on the sick for their healing, were stoned for their faith, endured persecution and imprisonment, kept in constant prayer, were beaten with rods and shipwrecked, and yet continually preached the Word.

But these things aren't that radical. We are just so far from normal that "normal" biblical Christianity seems radical to us. We must recognize that extravagance is a proportionate response.

A THOUSAND LITTLE YESES

When we think of bodily persecution and suffering, we can idealize and romanticize the thought of dying a martyr's death and receiving a crown of glory. One day, yes, the Lord may, in fact, graciously require us to give our very life unto death for His name's sake and demonstrate to us that nothing can separate us from His presence—even death (Rom. 8:38–39). But today and every day we have an opportunity to enter into the fellowship of His sufferings. We do not have to wait for a day of physical persecution to come in order to die to ourselves, our vain ambitions, and ungodly desires. We have the opportunity today to take up our cross and live the crucified and abundant life that He promised we could experience presently and constantly.

> I have been crucified with Christ; it is no longer I who live, but Christ lives in me; and the life which I now live in the flesh I live by faith in the Son of God, who loved me and gave Himself for me.
>
> —GALATIANS 2:20

A few years ago my family and I were leading our ACTS school on a short-term mission to a Muslim majority nation. We led a rather large team of about twenty young people, and our main purpose for this outreach was daily prayer and worship as well as daily evangelistic endeavors throughout the city. This was our second year directing the ACTS school, and we were feeling excited and encouraged in our efforts. The young

64

people were on fire with a vision to reach the unreached with the gospel, to plant praying churches, and to advance the kingdom to all nations so as to hasten the return of Jesus. I was giving exhortations almost daily on radical obedience and extravagant, sacrificial love for Jesus, and we were all burning with these messages.

Well, one night a few weeks into the outreach, as I settled into bed after a long day of leading team staff meetings, prayer meetings, and evangelism outreach, my wife decided it was a good time to bring up an important point. This was actually her first experience on an overseas mission, and since we had traveled as a family, she split her time on outreach with caring for our four-year-old and two-year-old and was pregnant with our third child at that time too.

She had been observing the team for several weeks and had a unique perspective within the midst of a majority of single twentysomething zealous missionaries. She said to me, "Brian, you know, you've done a really amazing job at giving these students a vision for the big yes. I honestly think most of these young people would give everything for Jesus, even to the point of death, perhaps. They own the vision for prayer and reaching the unreached. You've done an incredible job."

I felt my pride well up. She was right! They did own the vision. They were radical young pioneering leaders, and most of them had already committed to long-term missions work in the unreached nations. Things were going really well.

"But you know what I think you've done a really bad job of?" she continued.

Wait, what? I felt jolted out of my self-praise party.

"You've done a bad job of teaching them about the little yes."

"What do you mean?" I asked.

"You know, the thousand little yeses we have to make every day to simply love and obey Jesus," she said. "I've been noticing how our young people jump at the chance to lead a worship set or pray on the microphone, or how they rushed up to talk to the imam the other day. But Brian, the girls were arguing over the dumbest thing yesterday. Hardly anyone is volunteering to do dishes. The general attitude of the group is not abounding with servant-heartedness and selflessness toward one another.

"We can talk all day about the extravagant lifestyle of devotion to Jesus and the cost of discipleship and call them all to be martyrs for Christ, but how do you think we get there? We need to be simple Christ followers who choose to lay down our lives daily.

"I'm having to come home early every day from evangelism because our two-year-old needs a nap. Am I missing out on obedience to Christ? No, that sacrifice—that little yes to lay down my life, my own ambitions and desires—counts as extravagant love too. Following Jesus is not all about the big yes, Brian. It's the thousand little yeses that we are invited to choose every day that make us true disciples."

THE THOUSAND LITTLE YESES

She was right. This is the reality of discipleship. This is the reality of following Jesus. It's not simply a prayer that converts us. True conversion is the continual walking out of our salvation with fear and trembling. It's daily being conformed to the image of Christ (Rom. 8:29), picking up our cross, and following after Him.

Suffering for Christ is not only being beaten with rods or being thrown into prison. In our Western context perhaps one day we might experience these things, but today most Christians in a Western context simply do not experience suffering or persecution equivalent to that described in the Book of Acts. Still, as Christians, no matter the economical or political context we find ourselves in, we are invited into the promise of abundant life that comes as a result of laying down our lives.

Your choice to deny yourself, to refuse selfish ambition, self-seeking, and pride, is still a real yes to discipleship. Your choice to serve your brother, to choose humility and servanthood, matters. Your choice to refuse giving in to entitlement, anger, impatience, or strife is following Jesus. It's real love.

> The best training is to learn to accept everything as it comes, as from Him whom our soul loves. The tests are always unexpected things, not great things that can be written up, but the common little rubs of life, silly little nothings, things you are ashamed of minding one scrap.[3]
> —AMY CARMICHAEL

In theory we are all shooting for the big yes, that moment when we choose to break the alabaster flask, whatever that means, at any given time. For some, it's writing a one hundred thousand dollar check and funding missionaries to the unreached peoples of the world. For others, it's actually getting on a plane and going to those unreached. But the truth is, the thousand little yeses prepare us for those moments of big sacrifice.

The seemingly small, hidden choices you make in your heart are far more difficult to gauge and measure, but every yes to God is a result of His grace. And the grace of God given to endure persecution and even martyrdom is the same grace the Holy Spirit gives you today to live a holy and Christlike life in all you say and do. He has given you all you need for life and godliness. He has shown you the way in which to walk and to order your life, and He has a beautiful, awe-inspiring plan for His glory in your life.

THE GREAT EXCHANGE

In many ways Christianity can be summed up this way: *all of me for all of Him.* And somehow we still argue about that exchange rate!

When we realize our life is not our own and that there's great joy in laying down our lives and giving up our rights for His name, then there is no cost we would not pay, no sacrifice we would not make. He is worth it all. And the reward of eternity spent in His presence, partnering with Him in dominion and fellowshipping in the joyous, indescribably wonderful Godhead, is the joy set before us this side of time.

The fellowship with the resurrection of Christ is the most exhilarating, unimaginably wonderful promise of the Christian faith. But do we live in light of this reality? Do we live in the hope and promise of resurrection? Just consider the contrary. If the resurrection of Christ wasn't real, would it affect your life? If that reality wasn't true—if He never did rise from the dead and was right now *not* seated at the right hand of the Majesty on high—would it really affect your day-to-day life? It should.

It ought to be the case that if the resurrection of Jesus was not a fact of history, then our lives would not make sense, and we would be pitied by all. But most of our lifestyles mirror those of the rest of the general population. We bear no great and prevailing witness of faith in the coming of Christ. The resurrection means nothing to us in any kind of way that affects our everyday life.

Our lives do not scream transcendence. Our lives do not rest on a dependent hope in the return of Christ. In fact, our lives do not look much different than most unbelievers. When a Christian is confronted with sacrifice, hardship, or suffering, we don't know how to process it, and we resist it just the same as our unbelieving neighbor does, cursing God in our hearts. Oh, how deeply the American prosperity mind-set has affected our worldview! How ingrained in our minds and hearts this false gospel has become, ensnaring entire generations of believers in its grasp!

We think we deserve to be prosperous. We believe we deserve to be successful, happy, and rich. Working with young people—and older people too, for that matter—it has been my experience that the single greatest issue threatening true Christian living in the West today is the issue of entitlement. It is the lie that has laid root in our hearts and minds, that sense that we deserve something better, to the point that when anything negative occurs in our lives, our immediate reaction is, "Why did this happen to me? God, how could You let this happen? Do You even love me?"

In our hearts we think we deserve more from life, that we deserve to be happy and successful and comfortable. But this is opposite of what Jesus asks of us in becoming His disciples. This is opposite of what you should expect from life as a follower of Jesus Christ.

Am I saying that you will live a life void of happiness, success, and comfort? Of course not. But happiness, success, and comfort are not the goal. They are not our expectation from this life but rather in the age to come. In this life we ought to expect to face trials of many kind and to find our hope and security in Christ, His Holy Spirit, and His promised return.

A True and Living Hope

Life is not easy. It is filled with hardships, disappointments, debts, and disease. There are moments of sweetness and moments of sorrow, a thousand ups and downs in a single day, and that cycle never ends. But what differentiates the life marked by Christ's saving blood and the life that is not? Hope. The promise that every single moment of struggle and suffering that you experience in this life can be exchanged for eternal, incorruptible reward in the age to come.

It sounds too good to be true. It sounds unbelievable and almost cheesy. But it is more real than you can imagine. And living in this kind of hope will change your life. The Holy Spirit is the down payment we receive of this promise—fellowship with God, partnership with His kingdom rule, and communion in divine, holy, exhilarating love. He is our Helper and Comforter.

But how many of us are too busy running to comfort after comfort, to distraction after distraction, that we never even let ourselves experience the true comfort of the Holy Spirit that Jesus promised? Have you ever wondered if the lack of joy and peace you feel is not due to your life not being comfortable or successful enough, but rather that of being too busy in the pursuit of such so-called comfort that you don't allow yourself to be truly comforted by the Holy Spirit?

Jesus does not promise to make your life happy and easy. He promises you a hope, peace, and joy that exceeds the trials and sufferings of life. He promises an exchange. All of you for all of Him. Your weak yes and His sufficient grace. Your one life and His resurrection power. Your extravagant offering and His ravished heart.

Remember Jesus's response to Mary's extravagance? He said her story would be told wherever His story is told—and it is. His extravagant love and our extravagant response is the beauty and power of the gospel, provoking nations to jealousy and bidding thirsty souls to come and drink.

Your fasting, your prayers, your sacrificial giving, your service to the poor, your lifestyle fashioned after the Sermon on the Mount, your forgiveness, your humility, your meekness, the time you "waste" in prayer and study of the Word, your resistance to the carnality of the earth, your choices in favor of righteousness and purity, your commitment to preach the good news wherever you go—these are not easy things. Following Jesus is all-consuming. But the rewards are worth more than a thousand lifetimes of carnal pleasure.

> For a day in Your courts is better than a
>   thousand.
> I would rather be a doorkeeper in the house of
>   my God
> Than dwell in the tents of wickedness.
> —PSALM 84:10

In this psalm the psalmist is saying that even one day in the presence of true beauty, joy, and holiness is worth a thousand days anywhere else—that even to be a doorkeeper in the house of God is better than anything and everything the world could offer in comparison. This is the song of a ruined heart.

Our God is better and worth it all. What the world calls radical is actually just a reasonable response to His worth. What many would deem extravagant devotion is just an appropriate measure of response to Christ's immeasurable beauty.

So let the scoffers rant on about waste. We know and cherish this truth: He is better, and He is worth it all—all sufferings and trials, all hardships and woe. He redeems it all with the nearness of His Spirit and the promise of His return. Therefore, until we meet Him face-to-face and are transformed into His likeness, may our lives be a pleasing aroma to His heart and a signpost of His worth to all nations.

Reflection Questions

Jesus told us that following after Him would be extraordinarily costly. In what ways has following Jesus been costly in your own life?

Are there areas in your life that you have deemed "off limits" to God? Perhaps these are even hidden to you right now. Ask the Lord to shine His light in your life to show you areas that you need to surrender to Him.

Is there a risk that you can take to glorify God's name today? Maybe it's sharing the gospel with a work friend or classmate. Maybe it's giving generously or demonstrating love to a hurting family member or friend. What could be a costly gift you give to God today?

— — — — — — — — —

Father of glory, I ask that You would give me a vision of Your Son's great worth. Like Mary when she broke the alabaster flask, I want my life to be an extravagant response to His incomparable beauty. Give me grace by Your Holy Spirit to take up my cross, to follow You with my whole heart in every area of my life. I am a stranger in the earth, and I want my life to be a signpost of Your worth, my love poured out as a pleasing aroma before You. Consume me with passion for Jesus, and let my life reflect His worth. Amen.

Chapter 5

THE ANCIENT DREAM

LORD, remember David
And all his afflictions;
How he swore to the LORD,
And vowed to the Mighty One of Jacob.

—PSALM 132:1–2

MOST OF US, even us followers of Jesus, live lives of boredom, unfulfillment, intimidation, and resignation to mediocrity. Inherently we long to live lives of adventure, lives that make a lasting impact on the earth, lives that count in eternity. Yet too many of us remain heroes only in our own imaginations. We never take the next step of faith that leads to this glorious adventure, the promise of abundant life, courageous love, and pilgrim faith.

Amy Carmichael, the famed missionary to India, profoundly stated, "We profess to be strangers and pilgrims, seeking after a country of our own, yet we settle down in the most un-stranger-like fashion, exactly as if we were quite at home and meant to stay as long as we could. I don't wonder apostolic miracles have died. Apostolic living certainly has."[1]

Let that sink in for a moment. Isn't that true of your life? You were fascinated by Jesus, you said yes to His free gift of salvation, and you began the journey of discipleship—becoming conformed to His image. You died to your old self, refused the sins and fleeting pleasures of this world, and set yourself on a course to eternal pleasure and reward. You are a pilgrim. Even the act of professing your need for a Savior was a declaration that this world is not your home, not enough to save or satisfy you. You are made for more and you've recognized this truth.

But what now? Does your day-to-day life reflect this truth? Does your life scream transcendence? Do your choices testify of your pilgrim faith? The answer to these questions is a painful one. For most of us, the answer is a resounding no. No, we are not living lives that reflect the passion and power of the gospel of Christ. No, we are not living with purpose and courage. No, our lives do not testify that the things of earth do not satisfy us.

On the contrary, our Friday nights are spent the same way as our unbelieving neighbors. Our time and passions are spent in much the same way as all the rest of the Western world. Our priorities mirror those of our godless, materialistic culture. In short, if we are honest, we want the same things they do: health, wealth, and happiness. We crave comfort and ease just as much as the next guy. We grasp for pleasure with the same mindless need.

The American prosperity mind-set has deeply affected our worldview. How ingrained in our minds and hearts this false gospel has become, ensnaring entire generations of believers in its grasp! We spend our lives in pursuit of the façade, "grasping for the wind," as Solomon says in Ecclesiastes 1:17. And at the end of the day are we not just as dissatisfied, disillusioned, and empty as our unbelieving counterparts?

The American dream of prosperity and comfort is a shallow, unfulfilling pursuit. It is a dead end. And we would do well to avoid it, to fight against it, and to root it out of our hearts and minds. Why? Because there's a better dream. There's a promise for us that will not fail, that will not turn out to be a lie. The call to follow Jesus—and the promise of hope, abundant life, and glorious adventure that goes with it—is just as real and vibrant today as it was when it was first issued. The reward He promised to the faithful is still the reward He promises today. It is God Himself dwelling with men in unbroken, perfect, and fearless fellowship. This promise is the answer to the ache inside every human heart. And the pursuit of this dream of God for fellowship with man is the real adventure your heart craves.

A MAN WHO MOVES GOD

LORD, remember David
And all his afflictions;

> How he swore to the LORD,
> And vowed to the Mighty One of Jacob:
> "Surely I will not go into the chamber of my
>   house,
> Or go up to the comfort of my bed;
> I will not give sleep to my eyes
> Or slumber to my eyelids,
> Until I find a place for the LORD,
> A dwelling place for the Mighty One of Jacob."
> —PSALM 132:1–5

You want to talk about an impactful life, one that resounds with eternal significance? Look at David. In this psalm we find the psalmist (usually attributed to Solomon, David's son) invoking God's memory of David. Solomon knew that David's holy resolve to build God a house so deeply moved God that if Solomon could stir the memory of David in God's heart, he knew he could stir an even greater response from God to his own prayer.

Think about that—Solomon had a need before God in prayer, so he invoked God's memory of David in order to stir God's heart to move. Normally we are told to remember God's promises and His works, but in this instance God is asked by one of us to remember the dedication of a man. Solomon knew David had touched the heart of God in such a way that God could not restrain Himself at the mention of David's vow. It was as if David had somehow tapped into the unspoken secret of God's heart. He touched something in the heart of God that caused such an undeniable impact that other men knew that invoking his memory would trigger God's passionate response. Surely David's life testifies that extravagant devotion moves God's heart.

I want to live a life like that. I want my children to be able to pray, "Lord, remember Brian and all his afflictions," and that somehow at the mere mention of my name and the remembrance of my life, God would be moved.

Men are moved every day by the simplest things. But what moves God? What does God remember? The life of David was certainly not free of sin and failure. So what did he access in the heart of God that set him apart from the rest? What did David find that caused him to make such a radical response to God as a vow—a vow that was obviously costly, as Solomon mentions "all his afflictions"?

To answer, let's first think about vows in general. They are quite radical. More than a mere promise, a vow holds a measure of weightiness that is uncomfortable to our modern sensibilities. We reserve the term *vow* for something as permanent and serious as a covenant of marriage, that "forever, until death" kind of promise. That is what David did. He vowed. He swore to God. He made an "in sickness and health, no turning back, till death do us part" kind of promise to God.

And like any true vow, it is only found to be true when it is tested.

David bore affliction because of his vow. It created pressure and persecution in his life. He was misunderstood, he was scoffed at, and he was ridiculed because of his promise to God. But the afflictions were not bitterness to David. These were wounds of love, and love is always willing to bear any cost because it apprehends a higher vision than personal reputation and promotion. David was willing to prioritize God's presence far above all of his own comfort and opportunities.

David wasn't caught up like we are in fulfilling a version of the American dream or even a Christianized version of the American dream. He was caught up seeking God with all of his heart. This is what caught God's attention, and as a result, it's what left a lasting impact on the earth.

By making this vow, David was committing himself to live with undistracted focus and a holy resolve. He was committing himself to turn his eyes away from worthless things, fixing his eyes in fascination on the One whose eyes burn with holy flames of fire and passion for His people.

In contrast, our lives demonstrate a consistent bent toward distraction. With the advent of the Internet and social media, we are so connected to one another in superficial ways, but we are losing deep connection with the uncreated Sovereign of the universe. It is far too easy to get caught up in hundreds of little things that in the end won't matter.

I promise that you will never regret for one moment in your life the choice to wholeheartedly abandon yourself to God and His purposes in this generation. I promise you, when you stand before the Lord on that Day of Judgment, He won't ever say to you, "Man, you took Me way too seriously!" The truth is you can't take

God too seriously. You cannot live too abandoned to the purposes of God. On the contrary, if you take God seriously, He will take you seriously. The legacy of David teaches us this truth.

David's life is an invitation to all of us and gives us permission to live in such a way that moves God's heart. We cannot earn anything in salvation, but how we choose to live our lives can determine the experiences of our generation in encountering the fullness of God for us.

MY OWN LIFE CHANGED

I remember when this ancient dream first met me in my own context. It was about ten years ago. I was twenty-one years old and in Washington, DC, working with Lou Engle to establish a prayer room that focused on justice initiatives in our nation. I had graduated from college earlier in the year and planned to enroll in law school and pursue a career in politics.

It was nearing Christmas time, and most of our small prayer community was disbanding for the holiday season. But something came over me during those days. I can only describe it as a sense of desperation. A hunger for God so gripped my soul that I decided I would not go home to be with my family for Christmas but instead would give myself to fasting and prayer. I decided to stay in what was then our little prayer room and seek God. I had a blanket, a change of clothes, some water, and my Bible, and I spent that Christmas break crying out to God.

I was reading and meditating on this same psalm—Psalm 132—when it happened. I was mulling over the vow of David to build God a resting place on the earth when I was suddenly overcome with the presence of the Holy Spirit. I heard a voice as close to the audible voice of the Lord as my faith will allow me to believe.

The voice said, "Will you steward an ancient dream?"

I immediately understood this "dream" to be the heart behind the vow of David that I had just been reading and praying about. For a moment it was as if the dream of God's heart and the purpose of man's existence became clear to me, and suddenly my ambitions and career goals became utterly worthless. I knew in that moment what I wanted to pursue with my whole heart for the rest of my days. The vow of David became my own and has since become something of a North Star for me over the course of my life.

SETTLING THE ISSUE

So how do we live this way? Let me begin by saying there is power in a settled heart. If you make a vow to live for this ancient dream—a dream far different than the ones chased by the people around you—you will have to settle the issue that you are going to miss out on stuff. You have to come to terms with the fact that people will not understand you or value your life choices. Settle it. There is so much freedom and power in settling these things in your heart while you are young.

I remember Mike Bickle sharing a story with me of his own decision toward this. When he was a young man in his early twenties, he determined to spend every Friday night and Saturday night prayer and worship and studying the Word of God. He set aside these nights for the Lord because so many of his friends saw these two nights as a time for entertainment. He decided to act in the opposite spirit and determined to not use those nights for social events or to see a movie but dedicated them to seek the Lord in prayer and/or worship. He talks of that one choice as one of the most impactful decisions of his life as a young adult. He was spared from much temptation, distraction, and wasted time because of that one simple choice. He chose to say yes to an invitation to pursue the knowledge of God, and that simple yes was a thousand nos to lesser things. I'm sure his choice was misunderstood foolish or offensive to many at the time, but the fruit of that choice cannot be taken from him.

David's choice was not easy. It resulted in afflictions, testings, and trials, as does our choice to enter into the kingdom of God. But the fruit of that choice reverberates in scope far beyond what he could have ever imagined. I believe the depth of this generation's choice will determine their depth of encounter in God.

Purpose in your heart to move forward in God. Make a choice to pursue Him in a radical way. You may feel uncomfortable making a vow, but you can set your heart in a long obedience in the same direction. You can make real statements of obedience to God, and you can really stick to them in the grace of God. It's called perseverance. It's called faith. It's called a magnificent obsession.

THE PATH OF SPIRITUAL VIOLENCE

Now, there's a difference between changing your opinion and actually changing your lifestyle. If you choose to pursue God's presence the way David pursued God's presence, it is likely to be one of the most disruptive choices you will make in your life. This radical abandonment David had for God and His purposes makes for a great poster, but it's a very difficult lifestyle. There will be real sacrifice involved with this pursuit. It takes real resolve—in fact, such a measure of resolve that Jesus referred to it as violent, saying, "The kingdom of heaven suffers violence, and the violent take it by force" (Matt. 11:12).

Spiritual violence is not just an extra-passionate presence in prayer meetings. It's a lifestyle of holiness so radically opposed to the status quo and spirit of this age that it actually produces a measure of confrontation in the spirit. You see, although we receive the kingdom as a child, we advance the kingdom with holy resolve. Like that old song says, "I have decided to follow Jesus, no turning back, no turning back."[2] Paul the Apostle reminds us it takes the whole armor of God and, "having done all, to stand" (Eph. 6:13).

Live desperately in radical pursuit of the presence of God. You can't be too radical or imbalanced in this. If you're worried about being unbalanced, just remember that John the Baptist was unbalanced. He lived in a wilderness, ate locusts and honey, and devoted himself to a life of consecration as a Nazirite—and Jesus called him the greatest man born of a woman! (See Matthew 11:11.) We don't need more balance in the church. We need men and women possessed of God who are willing to pay any price, make any sacrifice, and give themselves wholeheartedly out of love for the Son of God.

A HEART-SIZE DWELLING PLACE

The vow David makes to build God a resting place is twofold. It is a corporate reality for the people as well as an inward, personal reality for himself. Both are crucial components to the tabernacle. They go hand in hand.

The personal element is no less important than the corporate dimension. In fact, the vow of David mentioned in Psalm 132 mirrors another heart cry he made to the Lord that's recorded in Psalm 101, where he says:

I will behave wisely in a perfect way.
Oh, when will You come to me?
I will walk within my house with a perfect
    heart.

I will set nothing wicked before my eyes;
I hate the work of those who fall away;
It shall not cling to me.
A perverse heart shall depart from me;

I will not know wickedness.

—PSALM 1101:2–4

David had such an ache for God, such a longing for unbroken communion, that he made a commitment to walk out his life in a perfect way. His desire to build God a resting place led him to commit to a holy life so that God would find a place of rest in his own human heart. He purposed that he would walk blameless before the Lord, that he would refuse to look upon worthless and wicked things, and that he would resist sin and carnality. He understood that the pleasures of the world, even the best "buzz" a life of sin had to offer, were simply not good enough in light of the joy found in God's presence.

Did David live a perfect life? Did he resist sin perfectly? We all know he didn't. He failed at many points in his life. But what David's life teaches us is that the persistent reach for God is pleasing to God. God is looking to respond to our longing. If we give an inch, He'll give a mile.

Speaking of the impact on God's heart from our persistent reach, let me tell you a story my father-in-law, Bob, loves to tell. Bob is one of the great men of God I know. Though he is not on a platform or serving in any formal sense of ministry, he is a man who consistently provokes me to simple obedience and hunger for God.

Bob is a decorative painter and works long hours each day in very labor-intensive work. But every night before he goes to sleep, he prays, "Before sleep finds my eyes, Lord, find a resting place in me." Then in his mind, he runs through the events of the day and spends time repenting, giving thanks, and just talking with God about all that happened throughout that day.

On one particularly hard day, as Bob tells it, he lay his head on the pillow and went through his normal routine of dialoguing with God. As he recalled the events of the day and how trying it was, he felt an extreme sense of shame and disgust in himself.

"Oh, God, I'm just so sorry," he cried out in prayer. "I did not represent You well today at all. I totally blew it today."

As he repented, he says he saw a big hand in the room with him. The hand held up one finger and then motioned, as if it was giving him a point on a scoreboard. He heard the Lord say in that moment, "Bob, for that, I'm giving you the whole day."

Bob immediately responded, "No you can't! You can't do that, Lord. I don't deserve that!"

"You're right, you don't deserve it," God said. "But I'm giving you the whole day anyway. Today counts as a win in My book."

My father-in-law tears up every time he tells this story, and usually there isn't a dry eye in the room when he tells it too. I share this story to illustrate how generous God is with us. His heart is turned toward us, longing to find a resting place in us. He does not disqualify us in our weakness or failure. Instead, He invites us in that very moment when we feel the weakest to receive His mercy and get back up in confidence in His call on our lives. He is looking for a heart reach, the longing that precedes lifestyle.

And what is so unbelievable about the mercy of God is that there is no way to earn it. It is a free gift. Mercy triumphs over judgment. We think we understand that concept, but there are so many circumstances where we would not give mercy, even to ourselves, but the Lord gives mercy. A couple of seconds of sincere repentance and He gives us the whole day.

God sees our hearts, and He responds based on our reach, not our failures. Bob reached toward God at the end of that difficult day, and it made all the difference. David may have sinned too, but he did not stay and wallow in that failure. He got back up. He ran into the mercy of God and renewed his commitment to that vision of the dwelling place of God.

Being a resting place for God is not about or based on our own determination but on understanding what God has already purchased for us. It's about getting caught up in the beautifully grand vision He sets before us. This propels us to live as we ought. Something David understood was the power of the mercy of God and lifting his focus off himself. David did not focus on his own ability to conquer sin or even on his ability to punish himself when he failed. In all things, victory and failure, he clung to the mercy of God. That is what God wants: dependence. A leaning and loving heart, focused on the great and abounding mercy and beauty of God.

Find a Grander Vision

When I talk with young men and women addicted to pornography or cycles of lust, I see their struggle primarily as an issue of vision and focus of life. Do they have purpose in life? Are they pursuing God whole-heartedly with passion and vigilance? Usually not. So the struggle with lust and pornography actually starts elsewhere.

Here too we can look to David as an example. Many people assume David's great sin was lusting after Bathsheba and the further sins that occurred after-ward—the lies and the murder. But David's first sin was actually disobedience to God's calling on his life. The passage in 2 Samuel 11 that tells us of David's affair with Bathsheba began with these words: "It happened in the spring of the year, at the time when kings go out to battle, that David sent Joab and his servants with him, and all Israel; and they destroyed the people of Ammon and besieged Rabbah. *But David remained at Jerusalem*" (v. 1, emphasis added).

In the spring when kings go to war, David stayed home. And while he was home, when he was meant to be at war, he walked out on the roof and gazed upon a woman who was not his wife, and he sinned. David made a choice of disobedience before he made a choice for lust. He was in a lazy, unfocused state of heart, and he set himself up to fall into temptation.

Again, a spiritual violence is necessary to live holy. You can't coast through life and expect to be holy and blameless. You must make hard, uncomfortable choices to pursue God first, to fulfill His calling with obedience, and to resist sin's temptations. It takes work and effort.

But the choice to resist sin is not fueled and sustained by our own determination. It is fueled and sustained by a vision of the supreme beauty of God. The way to maintain a holy life is to lift your eyes off yourself and your own ability, to cling to the mercy of God, and to get a vision—and continually renew that vision—of God's beauty.

Longing for God and the purpose-driven pursuit of Him produces holy living. When we live holy, God finds a place of rest in us. It's what set Noah apart in his generation. His holy life arose before the Lord like a soothing aroma in the midst of an exceedingly wicked generation.

God does not want to strive with men. He longs to come and walk with us in the cool of the day, not to find us hiding in our shame and sin. A commitment to build God a resting place in the earth is a very real commitment to personal holiness. The cry for God's unbroken, unhindered presence in the earth is a cry for that same presence in our own hearts.

The vow of David is a huge statement that business as usual is insufficient and irrelevant in light of God's desire. There's an urgency and a desperation in David's choice. With his vow, David was helping us see there is something more important, something far bigger than the American dream. That drive, that ambition, all that energy we spend in pursuit of self-profit? David deemed that end goal as folly and instead made a commitment to something greater, albeit foolish and wasteful in the world's eyes.

But to David it was not a waste, just as to Mary of Bethany and to Paul the Apostle it was not a waste.

Most of all, to God it was not a waste. On the contrary, these are the ones in history who are remembered by us and by heaven, weak and broken human beings who made lasting and significant impact.

Radical devotion, vows of passionate resolve, and love-sick obedience are illogical in our current context. So again, you can expect to be misunderstood, scoffed at, and ridiculed. But is a servant greater than his master? Isn't this the way that Jesus walked? What joy of communion might you experience, should you choose this lonely road?

It really is worth it. There is a payoff, but it's not in gold and silver. If we will choose to live this way with the Lord, He will come and make His dwelling place among us. We may not receive material prosperity, but we will experience something more grand—the presence of God in a manifest and very real way.

THE DREAM OF GOD'S HEART

God too has a dream in His heart. Yes, for your life, your ministry, and your personal good. But even more than that, He has a dream for His own glory to be manifest in the earth. He has a dream to be seen and loved by all nations, tribes, and tongues. And He has a dream to live and dwell with men in the joyous fellowship we were originally intended to delight in and experience in the Garden of Eden.

Whether you perceive it or not, your life is not a singular entity. You were not created to live and exist within your own comfortable bubble. Your life has been written into a greater story line—a story of a passionate, creative, holy, and lovesick God who longs for vibrant relationship with His children so that He might manifest His glory to all the earth.

And even now His Holy Spirit is moving across the earth. He is preparing, inviting, and awakening hearts to this greater vision. He is stirring us to live lives of radical pursuit, lives devoted to one thing. He is teaching us a new song, a song of lovesick longing— "Come, Lord Jesus, come"—because this was His plan of redemption all along: no more separation. He wants the garden again. He wants communion again.

This is why a young man or woman who makes this vow as David did will change the world. Because God is searching and longing for a heart that is loyal, that is devoted, that is longing for Him. But in order to do what? To give them a few goose bumps in a worship service? To give them a few good tweets? To give them an enjoyable prayer meeting? Those are all good things, but no. He is after more than that. God's longing is deeper than those things. He wants to show Himself strong, to display His glory, and to draw near to the loyal hearted.

The truth is, we have yet to see the steel punch of God revealed in this generation. We have yet to see a national, coast-to-coast, north-to-south awakening. And I don't just want to experience revival from the sidelines. I want to have a part—even just a small part—in seeing revival touch our generation. Don't you? When John the Baptist died, Jesus said he was a "burning and shining lamp, and you were willing for a time to rejoice in his light" (John 5:35). Don't settle to just rejoice in someone else's light for a little while. Actually be a burning and shining lamp that is fully surrendered to God and His purposes in our generation.

Yes, I believe God's intent looks like revival, that it looks like signs and wonders, souls getting saved, and healings and deliverances. But it also looks like young men and women walking in righteousness in the midst of a wicked and perverse generation. It looks like a mighty and prevailing prayer movement rising up across the earth and in every nation. Ultimately, it looks like God coming back to the earth. His desire is to literally dwell with men. He wants to come back. Jesus wants to come back. This is what He is doing in the earth. This is the call of the Holy Spirit to you today, to dream a bigger dream than the empty, fruitless shell of hope the American dream presents to you.

I challenge you to get a vision of the dwelling place of God with men. Purpose your heart to live in light of this eternal desire in God's heart, and make your life's primary ambition to build God a resting place on the earth. For some this will mean becoming full-time missionaries to the ends of the earth. For others it will mean becoming doctors, lawyers, and politicians. My point is that this is more than a career choice. This is a heart and life set after God's own heart. When God's dream becomes your own, it transcends vocation. It is a heart and mind-set change that, from the inside out, impacts every fiber of your being and ultimately the world.

REFLECTION QUESTIONS

When you examine your life, in what ways are you living in pursuit of the American dream?

What are some practical ways you can say yes to pursue the dream of God's heart with your time, energy, and resources?

In what way are you giving yourself to building God a resting place, both in a corporate and personal reality?

— — — — — — — — —

Lord, today I ask to be filled with the knowledge of Your will in all wisdom and spiritual understanding. Reveal to me what You are thinking and feeling. When You see the earth and when You look upon my heart, what do You desire? I want to be consumed with Your vision and desire. I want the dream of Your heart to consume me. I pray that I would live a life that is fully pleasing to You. I pray that You would find a resting place in my heart and in the earth. As David did, I commit to put aside my own pursuits and ambitions, and choose instead to build You a dwelling place in the earth. Make this my primary heart cry. Amen.

Chapter 6

OUR GREAT HELPER

And I will pray the Father, and He will
give you another Helper, that He may abide
with you forever—the Spirit of truth, whom
the world cannot receive, because it nei-
ther sees Him nor knows Him; but you know
Him, for He dwells with you and will be
in you. I will not leave you orphans; I will
come to you.... The Helper, the Holy Spirit,
whom the Father will send in My name, He
will teach you all things, and bring to your
remembrance all things that I said to you.

—JOHN 14:16–18, 26

W E CANNOT LIVE for God in our own strength.
In light of all that we have been called to and
the necessity we have to walk out this call in faithful
obedience, we need His help. Any time that I think I

can live in obedience to Him by myself, I fail miserably. Trying harder is rarely enough.

Yet these are the beautiful boundary lines that God places around every heart whom He calls. He leaves very little room for strife or making it work all on our own. He didn't set up His kingdom to be a network of obedient little minions to do His bidding without question or thought. He set up His kingdom as a dynamic flow of relationship with weak and broken human beings, that He might display His glory as a God of kindness and immeasurable mercy.

Paul emphasizes this truth in his appeal to the Gentile believers in Athens:

> God, who made the world and everything in it, since He is Lord of heaven and earth, does not dwell in temples made with hands. Nor is He worshiped with men's hands, as though He needed anything, since He gives to all life, breath, and all things. And He has made from one blood every nation of men to dwell on all the face of the earth, and has determined their preappointed times and the boundaries of their dwellings, so that they should seek the Lord, in the hope that they might grope for Him and find Him, though He is not far from each one of us.
>
> —ACTS 17:24–27

Here, Paul is emphasizing the divine interaction of the Godhead with the sons of men. God is involved in our lives, setting up boundaries and seasons in them, all in an endeavor to produce a longing and reach for Him in our hearts. Every season, every scenario in our lives, the good and bad, the difficult and the enjoyable, are all a beautiful strategy of God to draw us unto Himself, that we might reach for Him, responding to His love.

In the life of the believer this response to God's love does not culminate in the sinner's prayer. Rather, the acceptance of God's salvation is the start of a greater journey of relationship with Him. As we grow in faith and maturity, we come to find that we do not need God less and less, but rather more. Our lives become a process of increasing dependence upon God. This just reinforces the contrasting reality of God's kingdom to that of our own earthly reality of growing in maturity. In our earthly reality, growing means becoming more and more independent. But in God's reality, as we grow, we lean. As we mature, we cling all the more. Our need for God becomes clearer with each passing season.

Yet our natural inclination toward strife and independence from God remains a warring faction in the battleground of our faith. We cannot strive our way into spiritual maturity. We cannot grow closer with God while seeking to be free of our need of Him. This is His wisdom. He invites everyone, but you must become as a child. And as a child, in utter dependency, unable to accomplish even the most basic of tasks apart from the aid of an elder, God grows us in loving, consistent participation with His Holy Spirit.

The invitation into intimacy with God and the charge of the first and great commandment to love God with all our heart, soul, mind, and strength is an invitation marked by dependency. We are charged to love God, but the reality of the matter is that we cannot make ourselves love God. We need God to help us love God. We need the Holy Spirit to help us and guide us into all truth. Our growth in God is a growth of dependence on His grace. And the Holy Spirit is the ever-present Helper, the nurturer and guide, the best friend and companion, more present and involved than we would ever dare to admit or perceive that we needed.

The beautiful thing is that the Holy Spirit loves to make us fall in love with Him. If we just ask Him to help us, the Scriptures promise that He will. Unfortunately, so few of us think to ask Him to help us, leaving us frustrated and bewildered, as we assume that obedience to the Word is only a fairy tale and completely unattainable. Our bent toward strife is so ingrained in us, it is so foreign to our minds to grasp that He is able and willing to help us whenever we ask.

But an abundant feast is prepared before us to satisfy our hunger. We are brought to a fountain that never runs dry, that our thirst would be quenched. We must only partake of the feast! We must only come and drink!

Paul tells us we've been "blessed...with every spiritual blessing in the heavenly places in Christ" (Eph. 1:3). Peter tells us God's divine power has given us all things pertaining to life and godliness, or all things pertaining to living a godly life (2 Pet. 1:3). If this is true, then in reality—beyond what we necessarily feel or experience on a daily basis in our lives—we have everything we need to live a godly and pleasing life unto God. His very

Spirit is at work in and through us to glorify God and conform us into His very image.

WHY ISN'T THIS REAL FOR US?

I am convicted that too often in our lives and churches, the Holy Spirit has been reduced to mere doctrine and that therefore no emphasis is given to building a powerful, dynamic relationship with this third Person of the Godhead. This is particularly staggering in light of the fact that Jesus spoke of the Holy Spirit with such specificity. He told us the Holy Spirit is our singular aid for walking out our calling as disciples. So much positive emphasis was made by Jesus concerning the coming of the Holy Spirit that Jesus actually said it was to our advantage that He go away from the earth, so that the Helper would come (John 16:7).

If having the Holy Spirit really makes things better, do our lives reflect that? If Jesus being gone, if this "distance" we feel from Him, this injustice of His absence, really is to our advantage, do we live like it? Do we live with the promise, the power, and the infilling of His very Spirit? Are we walking in the joyous fellowship and power that Jesus promised would come to those who received the Holy Spirit?

A life set apart in passion for Jesus and wholesale obedience and devotion to His Word is absolutely possible in this life. It is not only possible, it is promised. What is even harder to believe is that it is actually His great joy to be the Helper. And it would be our joy as well if we would open ourselves up to the relationship. The Holy

Spirit of God is given as a seal, a down payment, an active, life-giving witness of our eternal identity as sons and daughters of God. He is more alive, more involved, more willing and able to help us than we dare imagine.

A vibrant, abundant life in the Spirit is absolutely available to us today. Unfortunately, our view of the Holy Spirit is often simply too small.

HOW TO LIVE WITH THE SPIRIT

I wonder if part of the reason so few believers pursue a vibrant relationship with the Holy Spirit is because of an ignorance on how it all actually "works." So first, it's important to understand how God created our human frame and how He designed us to relate to Him in real-time communion and fellowship.

God created us in three parts—spirit, soul, and body. Our inner man, or the hidden person of the heart, is comprised of spirit and soul (our mind, emotions, and will), and our outer man is our physical body. We see this demonstrated throughout Scripture:

> May your whole spirit, soul, and body be preserved blameless.
> —1 THESSALONIANS 5:23

> Our outward man is perishing, yet the inward man is being renewed day by day.
> —2 CORINTHIANS 4:16

> Do not let your adornment be merely outward...let it be the hidden person of the heart,

with the incorruptible beauty of a gentle and
quiet spirit.

—1 Peter 3:3–4

"Out of his heart [the NAS says 'innermost
being'] will flow rivers of living water."

—John 7:38

The distinction between the inner and outer man is an
important one. As humans, we so often look for our experiences in the physical, tangible dimension. We gauge our
lives and even gauge God by how much we feel His presence or hear His voice. One of the greatest struggles—but
important steps—in the life of the believer is breaking
down this expectation that everything with God will be
easy and loud and undeniable.

The interior world, the hidden person of the heart, is
the arena where God has chosen to display His glory
in us. Everything we are and do flows out of this interior reality. Yes, the move of the Holy Spirit is usually
thought of and talked about in terms of outward, physical demonstrations of His power—we hear of revival in
the nations, of anointed worship, of charismatic behav-
iors in church meetings—and those are all real and
powerful demonstrations of His move. But I believe
there is no greater demonstration of the power of the
Holy Spirit than when a person's heart is changed from
the inside out.

God has always been looking into the hearts of individuals, and He is intricately involved in and interested
in perfecting and sanctifying us from the inside out.

Again, this is beyond our own doing and human attainment. The power and grace of God alone is what truly changes a human heart, and the world "behind the face" is where He has chosen to move in His daily, present-tense demonstrations of power.

So, here's how it works. At our new birth of conversion, the Holy Spirit comes to live in our spirits. In that moment the uncreated life of God begins to dwell in our very frames. Paul says, "He who is joined to the Lord is one spirit with Him" (1 Cor. 6:17). This means God deposits into our spirits the seed of His very being. This is one of the most staggering, incomprehensible, beautiful mysteries of God! Books and books could and should be written on this subject. Hours of thankful meditation should be given to this matter. The fact of God's very Spirit dwelling within us—not just near us or beside us or responding once we cry out—is the treasure and mystery of God's goodness and love for us.

One purpose for the indwelling of God's Holy Spirit in us is to destroy the works of darkness in us. We see this in 1 John 3: "For this purpose the Son of God was manifested, that He might destroy the works of the devil. Whoever has been born of God does not sin, for His seed remains in him" (vv. 8–9). In other words, we have received within our spirits the very same power that raised Jesus from the dead, the same power that overcame the grip and penalty of sin in our lives, which is death. It is a power that overcame death—that defeated death when Christ rose from the dead. This same power is at work within us, working to cleanse us, sanctify us, and enable us to live holy lives—to be holy as He is holy.

Jesus is a high priest according to the power of the Spirit, who is described as indestructible: "If another priest [meaning Jesus] arises according to the likeness of Melchizedek, who has become such...according to the power of an indestructible life" (Heb. 7:15–16, NAS). In other words, the Spirit has power to destroy all the lust and darkness that opposes Him. Nothing can come against Him. He is indestructible. And at our new birth, we received the Holy Spirit, or the power of God's indestructible life, within our very frames.

This is the power available to us! It is a power strong enough to war against the works of darkness, both in the world and in our own hearts—and win! Yet most of us live intimidated by our sin, feeling helpless and weak in our attempts at holy living.

My brothers and sisters, it should not be so.

Of course, I don't mean to downplay the gravity of sin here, but I do believe we pay far too much attention to sin than we do the power we possess to conquer it. If the very same power that raised Christ from the dead is living within us, then we have more than enough power to resist the temptation to sin. We have the antidote to the poison of sin, in fact, and it's the power of the Holy Spirit of God living and working within us. We must only partake of Him.

How do we do that? Paul tells us:

> I say then: Walk in the Spirit, and you shall not
> fulfill the lust [sinful desires] of the flesh. For

the flesh lusts [wars] against the Spirit, and the
Spirit against the flesh.

—Galatians 5:16–17

In this passage Paul describes our fellowship with
God's Spirit in very raw, even aggressive language. He
paints an imagery of the "before" and "after" scenario
of a life filled with the Spirit, and it's a life of slavery
versus a life of freedom and abundance. The "flesh" in
Paul's theology includes sinful physical pleasures (sensuality, gluttony, alcoholism, etc.) as well as sinful emotions (pride, bitterness, anger, defensiveness, etc.).

Here Paul describes the relationship between our
flesh and the Spirit of God as a violent war inside every
believer. The flesh wars against the Spirit, and the Spirit
wars against the flesh. But this spiritual battle is not
automatic. There is no such thing as "coasting" in our
walk with God. A necessary measure of agreement and
active engagement is required for every believer.

Paul exhorts us that the way to wage war against the
lusts of the flesh, both physical and emotional, is to
walk in the Spirit. Paul then follows this teaching with
one of the great promises in Scripture: "You shall not
fulfill the lust of the flesh." We are not promised that
all fleshly desire will be gone, nor that the war will be
over, but that we will have power to not fulfill or walk
out our sinful desires. We are given the power to say no
to sin every single day, every single moment. We have
access to a holy and abundant life in God, free from
the weight of sin, but we will only walk in this measure

of freedom to the degree that we walk in the Spirit, or keep fellowship with Him.

When you examine your life, then, how much freedom and breakthrough are you walking in? How much are you walking out your life as a vibrant relationship with the Holy Spirit? It is given as a free and open invitation to every believer, but it is a choice we must make on a daily, even moment-by-moment, basis. The attack of the enemy on our lives does not stop. The battle for our affection is unceasing, and the single most powerful weapon you and I have against this onslaught of darkness is to walk in the Spirit.

Again, how do we do this? By talking with Him. The fundamental way to walk in the Spirit is by maintaining an active dialogue with the indwelling Spirit of God in us. This is key to our transformation and renewal. It is so simple that it causes many to miss it. Most of us are subconsciously expecting or looking for some once-in-a-lifetime, world-shaking encounter with God that allows us to walk away changed. The Holy Spirit makes Himself so available to every single human heart, we usually miss it completely in our hunt for some spectacular event.

The best part is, if we talk to Him, He will talk back! He will speak to us once He gets us in the conversation. How? By giving us impressions that release power on our minds and hearts if we respond to them. By talking us out of sinning and quitting. By giving us peace in moments of anxiety. By giving us courage to follow and obey Him in real time, like when obedience to Him looks like emptying the dishwasher for your wife or giving a thousand dollars to missions work or forgiving the person who betrayed you or turning off the computer when you are tempted to browse an indecent website at night.

If we simply talk to the Holy Spirit, making our lives an ongoing, unbroken conversation with God, we will experience the flow of relationship with Him that we long for. It really is that simple. But we will not walk in the Spirit more than we talk to the Spirit. He will help us to the degree that we talk to Him. The moments that we dialogue with Him are the moments in which we are most aware of His power in our inner man. Talking to Him releases that power. In those moments we turn the temptation into a conversation, when we ask for grace in the very moment we need it, He releases power on our minds and hearts. It doesn't usually come in an angelic visitation or a sudden surge of godly desire. Nevertheless, the power is real in the whisper, in the conviction, in the peace we receive.

We experience the Spirit's power in small, incremental ways, just like we do with food and water. God designed the process of sanctification to be exactly that—a process. Our Christian walk is, as I've said before, a continual growth of dependence, a perpetual dialogue with God. This is what I think Paul was referring to when he commended all believers to pray without ceasing (1 Thess. 5:17). He wasn't telling us we have to be in constant warlike intercession, but rather in constant dialogue with and awareness of the nearness of God, who is ever willing to strengthen and empower us in our faith.

We need to focus on the presence of the indwelling Holy Spirit in our war against sin. While many put their primary focus on the necessity of denying sinful desires, walking in the Spirit is an essential condition in overcoming lust. We cannot resist sin out of willpower alone. The way we remove darkness is by turning on the light.

I love the analogy Mike Bickle gives on this principle. He describes the battle against sin as being in a dark room and trying to get rid of the darkness by scooping it out with a cup. It'll never work. Instead, you must simply turn on the light. Then the darkness will be dispelled in an instant, because light is more powerful than darkness. Like John tells us, "Light shines in the darkness, and the darkness did not comprehend [overpower] it" (John 1:5). The key to overcoming areas of sin and darkness in your life is to fill yourself and those areas of your heart with brilliant light.

A MORE POWERFUL LAW

> I find then a law [principle], that evil is present with me, the one who wills to do good. For I delight in the law of God.... But I see another law [principle] in my members, warring against the law of my mind, and bringing me into captivity to the law of sin which is in my members. O wretched man that I am! Who will deliver me from this body of death? I thank God—through [ongoing encounter with] Jesus Christ our Lord!

> ...For the law of the Spirit of life in Christ
> Jesus has made me free from the law of sin.
> —ROMANS 7:21–25; 8:2

The law of sin that Paul describes in the above passage does not suddenly disappear when we pray the sinner's prayer, but its power over our lives is broken, and we receive the weapons and grace needed to overcome it. For example, one day our minds may be confused. The next day our emotions may be enraged. The next day our bodies may be tired, sick, or stirred up with sinful desires for immorality, alcohol, drugs, or food. When we choose to make these battles against sin a moment of encounter and dialogue with the Holy Spirit, He releases energy, healing, and righteousness in our mortal bodies:

> If Christ is in you, the body is dead because of
> sin, but the Spirit is life because of righteousness. But if the Spirit of Him who raised Jesus
> from the dead dwells in you, He...will also
> give life to your mortal bodies through His
> Spirit who dwells in you.
> —ROMANS 8:10–11

A law is an activity that happens in a consistent way with the same results. It is a principle that has been proven to hold true and functions in the same way each time. For example, the law of gravity works 100 percent of the time unless a greater law is introduced. When the engine of an airplane has fuel and is turned on, then it overpowers the law of gravity by activating the law of aerodynamics.

The law of the Spirit of life speaks of the consistent principle of the Spirit's power in us that is stronger than the law of sin referenced in Romans 8:2. The law of sin has dominion in us unless we engage in a more powerful law—the law of the Spirit of life. God has provided this more powerful law, but we must talk with the Spirit to experience its power. Our deliverance only comes as we encounter Jesus in an ongoing way by the Spirit (Rom. 7:25).

The point is, the law of sin does not disappear just because we try to ignore it. We overcome it by continually engaging with a greater power, a stronger law.

Furthermore, you cannot depend on past encounters to carry you through today's battle. God gives you fresh grace each day and each moment you ask for it. Just as a pilot must keep the engines running at all times to overpower the law of gravity, not resting in the plane's track record of successful flights in the past to keep the plane in the air if the engine isn't running, our authority is found in our current, ongoing, present-tense inner life with the Spirit.

THE THOUGHT WAR

Our thought life is a powerful, secret world nestled behind all that we say and do. You never really know what someone is thinking. What we dwell on in our thoughts actually has the power to direct our actions. If a person allows themselves to lust on a regular basis, perhaps thinking it is harmless to just think about the inappropriate fantasy, rather than act it out, they will eventually be emboldened to act upon that thought. If a person allows themselves to grumble and complain in their thoughts, they will eventually speak out that complaint or lash out in anger.

Our thoughts are not a disjointed entity from our actions and desires. What we allow ourselves to dwell on in our thought life influences what we say and do. This is why we are exhorted in Scripture to take every thought captive (2 Cor. 10:5) and to set our minds on things above (Col. 3:2). When we focus our drifting thoughts on something good, pure, and life-giving, we are actually strengthened to live righteously.

The mind set on the flesh has two expressions. First, it is overtly sinful. Second, it is preoccupied with the natural processes of struggle and conflict rather than the Spirit's process. A mind set on the things of the flesh is given to worry, fear, and insecurity, while a mind set on the Spirit is filled with peace, confidence, and courage.

So then, we live according to the Spirit by simply and literally setting our minds on the Spirit. Paul teaches this principle in Romans 8: "For those who live according to the flesh set their minds on the things of the flesh, but those who live according to the Spirit [set their minds on] the things of the Spirit. For to be carnally minded is death, but to be spiritually minded ['the mind set on the Spirit' in the NAS] is life and peace" (vv. 5–6). This is what it means to be spiritually minded, or to be mindful of the Spirit, or to be mind-filled with the Spirit. It's a simple concept, but it's amazing how many people miss it in the day-to-day grind of life. When we think about God, when we make Him our daydream, power is imparted to our inner man, strengthening us to live godly and pleasing before Him.

It's as simple as redirecting our thought life to God, then. How does that happen? Again, one of the easiest ways is to create a conversation with Him. The moments we dialogue with God are the moments in which we are most aware of His power and presence in our inner man. Talking to the Spirit redirects our focus from human fantasy to godly reality.

When we sin, we quench the Spirit, and the awareness of God's presence and grace in us is diminished. But when we turn the temptation into a conversation, when we turn our wandering into a reach, we will access His powerful grace to resist sin. The Holy Spirit in us is greater than the devil and the flesh (1 John 4:4), but His power works in us only as we actively engage with Him by speaking to Him.

When you're facing the temptation to lust, to complain, to lash out in anger, to gossip or slander, or to enter into any other sin, talk to the Holy Spirit. He is with you to help you. He delights in making you holy. He will give you the grace in that moment to resist sin and choose godliness, and He will awaken love in your heart, growing you up in confidence and maturity.

The Cry for More

While the Holy Spirit's primary work in the life of the believer is internal, His power and grace should and will flow out of us in a marked and tangible way. His joy is conforming us to the likeness of Jesus, both to present us blameless and pleasing before God the Father and to display His glorious power and beauty to all the earth.

In other words, the Holy Spirit is not only subtle and hidden. Sometimes when He moves, it is undeniable and life-altering. There is a measure of the Holy Spirit we receive at the new birth, the indwelling Spirit who abides with us always, but there is also a measure of the Holy Spirit that we must also contend to walk in. It's what Jesus promises the disciples will happen if they tarry and wait for it to happen:

> But you shall receive power when the Holy Spirit has come upon you; and you shall be witnesses to Me in Jerusalem, and in all Judea and Samaria, and to the end of the earth.
>
> —Acts 1:8

Here, in referencing the Holy Spirit's power, Jesus refers to *dunamis* power, or dynamite power. This is explosive power. It's not subtle. It's not hidden. It's not invisible or subconscious. It's not something that happens to you in your sleep. It's not something that happens without your knowledge. When the Holy Spirit came to the disciples in the Book of Acts, it was visible and tangible. It came as a mighty rushing wind. They saw tongues of fire upon the heads of those who were sitting in that upper room in that moment.

The same can happen to you.

But in all reality, we can live a good Christian life, die, and go to heaven and never walk in this kind of experiential power of the Holy Spirit. It's not a matter of salvation. It is, however, an invitation to a richer, fuller expression of faith and fellowship with God. We can go on with our lives as they are, be saved, and attend church, but we will never experience the ability to pour our love out on Him to the fullest extent until we've experience *His* love toward us to the fullest extent that we can.

Encounters with the Holy Spirit produced what the mystics described as *ineffable love,* but it is not going to come by just good Christian living alone. It is going to come with a cry in our heart that says, "God, give us more! There must be more!" Our barrenness and inability to produce goodness and holiness in ourselves—or even to awaken love in our own hearts—should produce an ache and contending cry in us for more of God.

Don't let anyone talk you out of reaching for more of God's presence and power in your life. Don't let anyone, not even yourself, develop a theology of barrenness, an excuse to go on living satisfied with far less than what you have been promised by Jesus. I hate language that excuses us from experiencing the "more" of God.

The Book of Acts should redefine what normal is in our lives. That book was never meant to be a benchmark of what to reach for, but rather a demonstration of an everyday way of life for followers of Christ. Instead, we've created a theology that justifies our barrenness and our powerlessness, thus accepting it as reality.

Acts is not simply meant to be considered and reviewed as a historical account of the early church and the movement of the Holy Spirit. Its testimony should lay waste to any vestige of status-quo Christianity in our lives. It should be a provocation that compels us to live our lives under the leadership and power of the Holy Spirit. That book is not meant to be our ceiling but rather our foundation—the ground floor of the Christian life and experience. The testimony of the early church's allegiance to Jesus and His mission should destroy our cheap and plastic religion and produce in us a cry for a real and authentic relationship with the Holy Spirit who manifests His life through us. This should be the cry of our hearts: to experience the power of the Holy Spirit, both to make us holy and to display the holiness of God to all the earth.

Frankly, we have not even come close to touching the light God has made available to us by the power of the Holy Spirit. The Book of Acts should serve as a devastating but hopeful reminder that we, as the church in the West, are not what we ought to be.

The ache for more of God's Spirit is not an accusatory cry, as if He owes us more. Rather, it is an ache of love. "Why don't you come carry away what you have stolen?" went the prayer of St. John of the Cross. The cry for more of God is the cry of a ruined heart.

Remembering that the Holy Spirit is not a formula, an event, or a concept but a real Person, cultivate a real relationship with Him. Walk in communion with Him on a daily basis. Talk with Him. Become familiar with Him as a friend. Take risks with Him, trusting His words and stretching your faith. Make your life a conversation with the Holy Spirit. He is the present and prevailing witness of Jesus in the earth and in the very real depths of your heart. He is working in you and through you a good work which He will be faithful to complete. Trust this. Be confident in your heart and courageous in your faith in His faithful, transforming power in your life.

REFLECTION QUESTIONS

Do you have a real, day-by-day relationship with the Holy Spirit? Throughout the day and when facing moments of temptation to sin, do you dialogue with Him? What does that look like for you?

Do you find within yourself an ache for more of the Holy Spirit's power in your life? In what areas would you like to see more evidential power of His work in your life?

— — — — — — — — —

Father, I thank You for Your abiding presence in my life. Thank You for the Holy Spirit present, near, and at work in my life to present me blameless before You. Father, You said if I asked You for more of the Holy Spirit, You would not deny me. So today I ask You for more of Your presence in my life. I want to walk with You in unbroken fellowship with Your Spirit. I want the Holy Spirit to become my best friend, my dearest companion in this journey of faith. Increase my awareness. Let me live mindful of the Holy Spirit's constant nearness and power to help me choose righteousness and resist darkness. I ask for an increase of light on the inside to live uprightly, walking in the fruit of the Spirit and shining as a testament of the glory of Jesus. Amen.

Chapter 7

A HAPPY HOLINESS

Be holy, for I am holy.

—1 PETER 1:16

WHETHER WE PERCEIVE it or not, we are living in a war. The enemy is aggressively and tirelessly working to capture the attention of this generation. If we look around and truly assess the gravity of the current state of this generation, we see how we are plagued with casualties of this war. Rampant addiction to media and entertainment of all forms (not just explicit), sexual confusion, and the horrors of sex trafficking across the globe—in short, immorality and godlessness abound. And the majority of young people live largely unaware of the battleground upon which they live.

Yet to rightly live as a disciple of Christ, we must be able to discern the hour, the times, and the seasons in which we live. It's important to understand the sobriety of our time and be able to discern the enemy's schemes against this generation. In an hour of so much gray and the wide-scale sentiment that anything goes, we must be able to call good "good" and evil "evil." We are called to live as lights in the darkness, a people set apart for the purposes of God and His glorious kingdom. In the midst of a wicked and perverse generation, we are called to be a standard of righteousness and shine as an unshakeable signpost of the superior pleasures of knowing God. We are called to be holy.

THE JOY OF HOLINESS

The Lord calls us to holiness because He is holy. In being holy God has the highest, most pleasurable, and most exhilarating quality of life in existence. He dwells in what I call the beauty of holiness, and when we begin to dream of dwelling in unity with Him, our lives become reoriented in joyous fellowship with His beautiful holiness.

We truly experience the joy of walking with Him as we walk in holiness. Though many see holiness as the drudgery of self-denial, the truth is that holiness is the most pleasurable and exhilarating quality of life in existence. It is how God lives all the time, and He wants to share that life with us that we may enjoy the superior pleasure of life in the freedom of holiness. I love C. S. Lewis's no-nonsense remark on this: "How little people know who think holiness is dull. When one meets the real thing...it is irresistible."[1]

Holiness equips us to enjoy life together with God forever. We needn't approach it in a negative way, with dread and fear of boredom. The truth is that holiness does not keep us from pleasure, but rather equips us to actually experience it! The power of holiness frees us from the vain imaginations, defilement, and dullness of lust, pride, and bitterness. When we walk out a holy lifestyle, our hearts are liberated to experience the pleasures of knowing God, unhindered and unquenched by the ensnarement of sin.

Holiness is far from a life of drudgery. It is living with a heart that is vibrant in love for Jesus and people. The happiest, most contented and vibrant people I know are ones who have set themselves apart in lifestyles of holiness and devotion to God—a far cry from the holiness stereotype of being a sheltered, sulking, judgmental elitist. Holiness is *happy*. It's magnetic. It's the most alive and vibrant state of being a human heart can abide in.

Furthermore, holiness is what God calls us to live out—to live as He lives, really. In fact, Jesus is described in Psalm 45 as being the happiest man who ever lived, literally anointed by the Father with gladness more than any other man: "You love righteousness and hate wickedness; therefore God, Your God, has anointed You with the oil of gladness more than Your companions" (v. 7). Why? Because of His love for righteousness. Because of His holiness. The fruit of holy living is joy and gladness. Jesus displays this for us and invites us into His likeness.

HOW TO BE HOLY

In our pursuit to live holy, I believe there are two foundational truths. The first is that in order to live a holy life, we must be preoccupied with the superior pleasures of God. The second truth is that out of this preoccupation with the pleasures of knowing God, we must set ourselves on a hundredfold obedience. Comprehending and embracing these two truths will provide a foundation for living holy in the midst of a wicked and perverse generation.

1. Preoccupy yourself with superior pleasures.

There is a prevalent but untrue sentiment in the church that pleasure is wrong. When people hear the word *pleasure*, they associate it with sinful desires, but the truth is that God is the very author of pleasure. Psalm 16:11 states that at God's right hand are pleasures forevermore, and we were created to partake of this pleasure for all eternity. He created us to enjoy physical, mental, emotional, and spiritual pleasure.

Since our longing for pleasure is part of our created design, it must be satisfied. The longing will not go away, no matter how we may try to ignore it. For all eternity, even, we will still long for pleasure! The good news is that we will be infinitely and eternally satisfied in our resurrected bodies as we live in the fullness of God's presence. This is part of our great hope and reward in the coming ages.

Of course, in this age the devil tempts us with fleeting and counterfeit pleasures. He does this to distract us from the superior pleasure of encountering God. He seeks to draw us in with physical and emotional pleasures outside God's will. But here's the thing. These counterfeit pleasures cannot satisfy the deep longing within our spirits, and that's because the truest and greatest pleasures available to the human spirit do not come from the counterfeit pleasures of sin. The greatest of all the pleasures available to the human heart are found when God is revealed to us. When the Father, through the Holy Spirit, reveals Himself to us, our spirit is awakened, satisfied, and fascinated. We are exhilarated at the deepest levels.

The tragedy of giving way to the temporary so-called pleasures of sin is that it cheats us of experiencing the greater pleasure of knowing God. But when we do experience the true, surpassing joy of encountering God, we are liberated from the inferior pleasures of sin. In the light of God's holiness sin is seen for what it is: gross and detestable, a fall far short of the matchless beauty and joy found in Jesus. We become ruined for the real and disillusioned with the lesser.

Now, the Spirit knows and discerns the deep things of the Father's heart and mind (1 Cor. 2:10–12) and allows us feel some of what the Father feels, revealing His delight, His emotions, His thoughts, and His plans. When we receive the Spirit, we are given access to know all that we have been freely given by God. I like to think of it as the Holy Spirit leading us on a divine treasure hunt into the beauty of Jesus. He takes the things that Jesus is thinking and feeling and reveals them to us. This is divine entertainment at its highest.

Of course, it does not happen all at once. Instant gratification is the way of our culture, not the way of the kingdom of God. God doesn't just flood our minds and hearts with limitless knowledge of Himself all at one time. When God reveals Himself to the human heart, it *mostly* comes in whispers. You must bend in close to hear Him. He releases small measures of insight and inspiration from the Word, which tenderizes our spirits for a few moments.

These subtle but powerful flashes of glory are meant to be a regular part of our relationship with God. Over time this holy influence changes our lives, causing us to, in turn, live holy. That's why Jesus taught us to ask for daily bread. Our encounter with God is meant to be a daily experience of pleasure, satisfaction, and joy, leaving us dissatisfied with sin and hungry for more of Him. These daily encounters with God fuel our fascination and sense of awe of Him. Without a sense of awe in our relationship with God, we will live spiritually bored, and will be more vulnerable to Satan's tactics. A spiritually bored believer is weak. A fascinated believer is strong and has no need for things such as pornography, idle speech, or gossip.

God created us with a deep longing to be fascinated. We love to be awestruck. We love to marvel and be filled with wonder. This is how God designed us, carefully crafting within us the capacity for fascination. It's not something we can escape. It must be satisfied. It will not just go away over time, and it will not remain neutral. Our hunger for fascination will either be satisfied the right way in God or the wrong way by darkness.

The entertainment industry has identified and targeted this God-given longing in the human heart. It has exploited this God-ordained craving to its profit and our ruin. Bombarded with the flashing lights since infancy, entertainment has become one of the primary felt needs of this generation in the Western world. It consumes our time and attention. Now within our grasp 24/7 in handheld devices, it travels with us wherever we go. We're attached to it like a dying patient to an IV. And yet can any of us say we are satisfied? Our attention span has only shortened. Our thirst has only increased. And whether intentionally or not, we end up living from fix to fix in our addiction to media and the entertainment industry.

I remember Lou Engle sharing the story with me of a man of God from a third-world nation who visited America for the first time. Seeing the state of the church, he declared, "I feel sorry for you in America. Your king is materialism, your queen is entertainment, and your crowned prince is sports. Where I am from, we worship God!" While we all face a unique landscape of battles wherever we are from, the church in the Western world must resist the pull for our fascination in a uniquely aggressive way. We are given no break. The battle for our attention and ultimately our affections is never neutral.

Many approaches to pursuing holiness, then, place the emphasis of holy living on self-denial rather than fascination with God. Yes, it is biblical to call people to deny themselves of sinful lusts and pleasures, and we are admonished throughout Scripture to resist sin. (Related to this, see Appendix C for an example of a purity covenant.) However, the best way to overcome darkness is not by focusing on the darkness and just trying our best to resist it. The most practical and successful way to resist sin is to focus on "the light of the knowledge of the glory of God in the face of Jesus Christ" (2 Cor. 4:6). As we discussed earlier, you overcome darkness with light (John 1:5).

In the same way, we will not overcome the darkness of immorality, bitterness, or pride by focusing on it. The way to decrease the darkness in us is to increase the amount of light we receive and enjoy. If we change our focus to gaining more of the light of the superior pleasure of revelation of God, the light will overpower the darkness we find within ourselves.

The way to overcome sin, in other words, is not by simply resisting sin alone. It is also accomplished by actively encountering more of Jesus. He is the Savior. He is the One who cleanses us from sin and breaks the power of darkness. He is the One who lived the perfect, sinless life, and it is only through encountering Him, growing in intimacy and fellowshipping with His Spirit, that we are transformed into His likeness, from glory to glory, day by day, and grace to grace.

We cannot repent of our inherent longing to be fascinated. It is God-given. It was built into our design when God created us, as recorded in Genesis 1. However, we will only satisfy this longing to be fascinated when we are fascinated by revelation of Jesus.

The apostle Paul was fascinated by the knowledge of Jesus. It was key to his life vision, as we see in Philippians

3: "I also count all things loss for the excellence of the knowledge of Christ" (v. 8). He is comparing all the treasures of earth—the greatest buzz or the top new box-office release—as rubbish, garbage compared to the excellence of the knowledge of God. Paul tapped into a truer source of beauty, and it fascinated him on a deeper level than all he had tasted previously.

Paul's own life is an example that we can live from this place. We must be preoccupied with a superior fascination. We must live with that sense of marvel and awe in our relationship with God because it is what empowers our inner man. When we live with a sense of awe, it causes us to live with fascination and a deep sense of purpose. This is what best equips us to resist temptation when it comes.

We sin because we believe it will provide a pleasure that's superior to obeying God. The power of temptation rests on a deceptive promise that sin will bring more satisfaction than living for God. Scripture calls this the deceitfulness of sin (Heb. 3:13) or deceitful lusts (Eph. 4:22).

The call to holiness is the call to enjoy God by living fascinated. The battle for holiness is the battle to be preoccupied with the right thing and is ultimately won in the pursuit of knowing and enjoying God. The way forward in holiness is to become preoccupied with pursuing the knowledge of God. This will lead us to the pleasure of living truly and deeply fascinated.

2. Set your heart on a hundredfold obedience.

As our souls awaken to true fascination with Jesus and we experience the joy of knowing Him, we are empowered to love and obey Him. Jesus said, "If you love Me, keep My commandments" (John 14:15). This means that obedience to God is how we demonstrate our love for Jesus. In other words, obedience is love.

But part of God's gift to us is the fact that He pours the love of Himself into our hearts. We love and desire Him because He awakens that very love and desire. Therefore, the God who calls for our full dedication to Him is the very one who empowers us to give it.

When we establish our commitment to live in hundredfold obedience, we experience a dynamic spark in our relationships with God that we would otherwise never have known. There is a deep encounter between us and God that is experienced only when we seek to yield every area of our lives to God. There is a measure of blessing and grace released upon the human spirit only when our hearts are set to live in 100 percent obedience to God.

Holding back even one issue from the leadership of the Spirit hinders our ability to experience God fully. I have come to realize that 98 percent pursuit of obedience has a limited blessing. That last 2 percent positions our hearts to receive the joy of the Holy Spirit, igniting vibrancy in our inner man. There is a spark of the Spirit in our hearts as we reach out to Him and aim to live this way. We should not settle for 98 percent, but rather live with a vision for complete surrender and the fullness of encounter.

There's a big difference between attaining 100 percent obedience and just aiming or reaching for it. His blessings are not released after we casually reach for holiness, but when we set our hearts to *fully* aim for it. There is power in making this decision to pursue complete surrender to God. When we intentionally reach in our spirits to obey Jesus in literally every area of our lives—in our speech, our eyes, our time, our money—we actually experience a new dimension in the grace of God.

This is more than a casual commitment to God. I am talking about deciding on a specific goal to fully obey Him in every area of our lives. The very reach of our hearts to live this way has a dynamic impact on our emotions. When we settle the issue and make the choice to surrender to Christ, we open ourselves up to the response of God, which is sufficient grace, inexpressible joy, and pleasures evermore.

I consider some of the great men and women of God who have gone before this generation, setting an example for us of holiness and surrender to God. John Wesley spoke of his commitment to Christ and the necessity of setting ourselves in an intentional way to obedience in this way:

> In the year 1725, being in the twenty-third year of my age, I met with Bishop Taylor's "Rules and Exercises of Holy Living and Dying." In reading several parts of this book, I was exceedingly affected; that part in particular

which relates to purity of intention. Instantly
I resolved to dedicate all my life to God, all my
thoughts, and words, and actions; being thor-
oughly convinced, there was no medium; but
that every part of my life (not some only) must
either be sacrifice to God, or myself, that is, in
effect, to the devil.

Can any serious person doubt of this, or find
a medium between serving God and serving
the devil?[2]

Always remember how much the Lord values our
journey to grow in love. His Holy Spirit is committed
to perfect what is lacking in our faith and to present us
blameless before Him in love. He fully enjoys us as we
grow and mature in Him. As a good father delights in
watching his children grow, our good Father delights
in our journey of growth. Therefore, when we sin, we
repent with the knowledge of God's unconditional love
over our lives. We can confidently renew our resolve to
fully love Him in every area of our lives because even
in our weakness, God honors the reach of our hearts
back toward Him. The attitude and desire of the heart
is what He sees and what He blesses with a fresh experience of His grace.

When we set our hearts to love and obey God fully,
the Holy Spirit helps and strengthens us. God responds
to our weak yes with such generous grace. The psalmist
explained this exchange in Psalm 91: "Because he has set
his love upon Me, therefore I will deliver him" (v. 14).
The Holy Spirit's primary job description is the Helper.

He is near, willing, and powerfully able to help us every moment that we ask. As we walk with Him, communing and dialoging with Him throughout our daily routines, we will experience greater levels of breakthrough and victory in our battles.

We must not underestimate the power of our choices. God honors the power of our decisions. He has given us the ability to set our affections on anything that we choose. This is the gift God bestows upon us: the gift of free will in our journey.

Our decisions by themselves are not enough to change our emotions, yet they play an important role in the process of our transformation. When we change our minds, setting ourselves to righteousness, the Spirit changes our hearts and brings our emotions under His leadership. When we make the choice to love Him fully, the Spirit helps our hearts feel His love and love Him in return.

It is important to understand this because so many young people are waiting for their emotions to change first. They want to *feel* like choosing righteousness. But our emotions will be affected over time by the move of the Holy Spirit within us. As we exercise the power of our free will and choose righteousness, our desires and emotions become aligned with Him.

God created us with deep longing for our love to be wholehearted, and we cannot function properly until we have set our hearts to be fully His. Many believers seek security and fulfillment in God without being abandoned to Him. But you don't get to experience the miracle of walking on water until you decide to get out of the boat, even in the middle of a storm. You won't know the safety, faithfulness, and adventure of God until you abandon yourself to Him.

Half-hearted followers of God most often struggle with a sense of emptiness, burnout, boredom, and discontentment, and I've found this is because they have too much of God to enjoy sin and too much of sin to enjoy God. They've gone too far in God that they feel guilty when they sin, but they still live with too much sin that they don't experience the full joy and freedom in God. This is the worst way to live! It's certainly not how we are called to live.

Living short of a hundredfold obedience to God actually diminishes our glory as human beings made for encounter and joyous fellowship with God. Living in wholehearted abandon to God is God's gift to us. It is His invitation to experience the fullness of glory that He intended for the human race.

God is passionate and created us with the need to be passionate. We were created for the glory of love, and we soar to the heights of our human potential only when we set our hearts to fully love God.

There is nothing more satisfying than to know we are giving our all to God. His insistence on our full obedience is not due to His being an insecure narcissist looking for human affirmation. He knows that only in fully loving Him are we able to experience the fullness of what it means to be human. By requiring our full dedication and in helping us to sustain it, He enables us to experience inexpressible joy. God is entirely self-sufficient, yet He desires our love. He does not need us, yet He abounds in desire for us. As we express our desire for Him in our daily actions, we soar in the joy of love.

PRACTICAL PRINCIPLES OF HOLY LIVING

In order to experience the foundational truths of experiencing pleasure and living in a hundredfold obedience, we find three practical principles outlined in Scripture that help us attain the goal of holiness. Paul outlines these principles in order to help the church to understand holiness in a practical way:

> *Reckon* yourselves to be dead indeed to sin, but alive to God in Christ....*Do not let* sin reign in your mortal body, that you should obey it in its lusts. And *do not present* your members as instruments of unrighteousness to sin, but *present* yourselves to God as being alive from the dead, and your members as instruments of righteousness to God.
> —ROMANS 6:11–13, EMPHASIS ADDED

In this passage we find three principles: the knowing principle, the resisting principle, and the pursuing principle. We must know truth, resist darkness, and pursue God. All three of these principles are crucial to maintaining a life of godliness and cannot be exchanged for another. In each point it is vital that we cooperate with the grace that God gives us in order to fully embrace the call of holiness. These three practical principles described by Paul specifically reveal our role in agreeing with and acting on the grace of God.

1. The knowing principle

Paul describes the knowing principle, saying, "Reckon [or see] yourselves to be dead indeed to sin, but alive to God in Christ" (v. 11). In order to resist sin and pursue God in a right way, we need to know and understand certain truths. We must know who we are in Christ, what He did for us, and what we receive in Him.

As believers, we all received the gift of righteousness, the indwelling Spirit, and the authority to use the name of Jesus. We are to reckon, or see, ourselves as dead to sin and alive to God because of the finished work of Jesus on the cross and His resurrection from the dead. We must understand the truth about God's heart, that He is our Father and our Bridegroom.

As we grow in knowledge concerning the good things that are in us in Christ Jesus, our faith becomes effective (Philem. 6). In order to effectively resist sin, we must gain understanding concerning our faith. We do this by choosing the "one thing" lifestyle, pursuing the knowledge of Jesus diligently through prayer and study of the Word.

2. The resisting principle

The resisting principle is described thus: "Do not let sin reign in your mortal body, that you should obey it in its lusts. And do not present your members as instruments of unrighteousness to sin" (Rom. 6:12–13).

Through this, we come to see that it is not enough to just know who we are. We must also put knowledge into action by resisting inferior pleasures. We must not go to places, buy items, look at, or talk about that which stirs up our sinful passions. We must agree with the grace of God to actively resist anything that would hinder our love for Him.

3. The pursuing principle

Paul presents the pursuing principle, saying, "Present yourselves to God as being alive from the dead, and your members as instruments of righteousness" (v. 13). This means we must actively pursue intimacy with God and present our bodies as instruments that He can use to bless others as we serve them and release the power and presence of Jesus in their lives. We pursue serving with humility, ministering to people in the power of the Holy Spirit and relating to God and people with love.

In pursuing lives of holiness, it is vital that we live out the first and second great commandments, by actively pursuing God every day and being vessels of love and power toward others. A pursuit of holiness is demonstrated in a life of purpose and vision. When we are visionless and aimless, as we learned earlier, we give in to temptation much more easily than when we are purpose-driven and give our lives to the focused work of the kingdom. Now, all three of these principles must operate together in our lives. It is not enough to just resist sin and pursue God without knowing who we are in Christ. Likewise, it is not enough to pursue God at prayer meetings or on missions trips without actively resisting sin. It does not work to only know truth and resist sin without actively pursuing love for God and for people. These three principles were created to work in harmony in us.

In all this there is a divine exchange between humans and God in the pursuit of holy abandonment. God requires us to play a part by cooperating with Him in the grace of God instead of receiving His grace in vain. Paul expressed this when he said, "We then...plead with you not to receive the grace of God in vain" (2 Cor. 6:1). The Bible describes a division of labor, where God releases grace and we choose to cooperate with the grace He gives. He will not do our part, and we cannot do His part. Our part includes making quality decisions to deny ourselves, to feed our spirit on the Word, and to ask for help through prayer. God's part includes releasing supernatural influences. He releases His supernatural influence on our hearts so they are bent toward godly desires, on our bodies so they experience healing, on our circumstances so we experience provision and protection, on our relationships so we receive favor, and in our ministries so that we witness His work in the lives of others.

We must dialogue with God about the issues of our lives and submit our resources to His leadership every day. When we cooperate in the grace of God in this way, God will honor His part. God will not do our job, but He will help us if we choose to receive His divine assistance. We must be in cooperation with Him and His grace in order to experience the abundant life we desire.

Let me assure you that a life of holiness—one in which we love God in every area of our lives—is possible now. It's not a charge for the super-Christian. It's not a mandate for the future, when we are fully mature. It's not waiting for us on the other side of eternity. It begins today, step by step, choice by choice, yes by yes. We must choose to love God with all that we are, one moment at a time, because He loved us with all that He had. He loved us to the end.

Let us find ourselves fascinated by Him, then, experiencing the supreme spiritual pleasure of His love and living in a hundredfold obedience to His ways. Let us live holy and happy as we go, loving our God with all our hearts, all of our minds, and all of our strength.

REFLECTION QUESTIONS

When you consider the wickedness so prevalent in our culture, are there any areas of your life that you have agreed with the spirit of the age rather than the truth of God's Word? What are those areas in your heart that are in agreement with darkness rather than light? Take a moment to repent and ask the Lord to cleanse and renew you.

We live holy by knowing truth, resisting darkness, and pursuing God with intentionality. What are some practical ways you can set yourself to pursue the knowledge of God? What are some practical ways you can resist sin in your personal life? What are some ways you can live out your love and obedience for God with more intentionality?

Father, I thank You for the free gift of righteousness I have received because of Jesus's finished work on the cross. I thank You for Your Holy Spirit, present and working in my life to sanctify me body, soul, and spirit. And I thank You for the authority You've given me to resist the powers of darkness. Lord, I want to live filled with the light of Your Spirit. I want to live holy as You are holy and to experience the superior pleasures of knowing You.

Jesus, I ask that You would become my obsession. Fascinate me with Your beauty, become my daydream, my preoccupation, and my consuming passion. Lift my eyes from worthless things, and capture my heart with the excellence of Christ. I set myself to pursue You wholeheartedly. I set my heart to love and obey You in every area of my life. Let the light of Your love and beauty fill me, that I would be a holy vessel, set apart for Your glory. Amen.

Chapter 8

SINGING BACK THE KING

And this gospel of the kingdom will be
preached in all the world as a witness to all
the nations, and then the end will come.

—Matthew 24:14

W E LIVE IN the most unique timeframe in human
history. In fact, I would go so far to say we are
living in the most exciting season in redemptive history
since the days of Jesus. Missiologists tell us we are living
within reach of fulfilling the promise of Matthew 24:14 in
this generation, where the gospel of the kingdom will have
been proclaimed to every people group.

This is significant because it means we really may
have the privilege of being the generation that partners
with Jesus to bring a close to this age. Though I know
this is a controversial thing to say, Jesus commands His
people to know the generation and the hour in which

they're living (v. 33). He even rebukes His own generation for not knowing and understanding the times and seasons in which they were living and for not being able to discern the eternal significance of their hour of visitation: "You know how to interpret the appearance of the sky, but you cannot interpret the signs of the time" (Matt. 16:3, NIV). Thus, it is imperative we understand both what Jesus commands and requires of us in this hour of history.

JOIN GOD IN GOD'S WORK

So many young people ask the question, "What is God's will for my life?" I understand that question. However, I believe we need to find out what God is doing in our generation first and then throw ourselves wholeheartedly into it. Young people are desperate to make an impact in the world. In fact, we all dream of making a lasting impact with our lives. We want to leave something to be remembered for or, at the very least, feel a sense of purpose in our lives.

That desire in our hearts is not wrong. It's a God-given ache for purpose we possess. We were made to encounter God and to change the world as a result of the flow of our relationship with Him. We were created to have dominion over the earth, to express in real time the kingdom of heaven on earth.

But so often people seek to satiate their longing for impact and purpose by looking for a new thing—a cutting-edge concept or a new twist in theology. True and lasting impact, however, is not attained through an exciting new idea or a breakthrough strategy. The world doesn't need a new thing. Rather, a return to an ancient path is what will change the world. We don't need a new vision. We just need to do what Jesus already told us to do, which is to go forth into all nations.

The Great Commission is, as Hudson Taylor said, "not an option to be considered; it is a command to be obeyed."[1] We don't need permission to change the world, because the Great Commission *is* the great permission given to us to act in His name. By simply obeying the command of Jesus, we can change history.

One of the single most impactful, radical things a young person can do is to throw themselves into what God is doing in this generation, partnering with His Holy Spirit and His commands in Scripture, which transcend generations. The binding commandment of the last two thousand years and God's will for His people is both the Great Commandment and the Great Commission: to know God and to make Him known. A young person seeking a radical life of obedience to God must simply humble himself or herself enough to get in line with His Spirit's agenda in the earth, which is ultimately to kindle a fire of longing for Jesus and a cry in unison for His return.

A Song to Beckon the King

I believe one of the most important things the Holy Spirit is emphasizing in this generation is the explosion of worship and prayer in the earth. We are witnessing a burgeoning prayer movement bursting forth across the nations of the earth, particularly among young people who are no longer satisfied with once-a-week church services but long to encounter the presence of God daily in the context of community. Just as Isaiah prophesied many centuries ago, the people of God are reorienting themselves around their eternal identity as "a house of prayer for all nations" (Isa. 56:7).

The Scriptures prophesy that in the last days, the people of God will be a worshipping people and the church will be a singing church as we sing a new song that signals and initiates the second coming of Jesus and transitions us into the next age. We see a model of this in the New Testament, when the early church gathered in prayer, worship, and fasting and the Holy Spirit anointed them to go forth and spread the gospel to unreached regions.

Consider what John Piper says in his book *A Hunger for God*:

> The fasting in Acts 13 changed the course of history. It is almost impossible to overstate the historical importance of that moment in the history of the world. Before this word from the Holy Spirit, there seems to have been no organized mission of the church beyond the eastern seacoast of the Mediterranean. Before this, Paul had made no missionary journeys westward to Asia Minor, Greece, Rome, or Spain. Before this Paul had not written any of his letters, which were all a result of his missionary travels, which began here.

This moment of prayer and fasting resulted in a missions movement that would catapult Christianity from obscurity into being the dominant religion of the Roman Empire within two and a half centuries, and would yield 1.3 billion adherents of the Christian religion today, with a Christian witness in virtually every country of the world. And thirteen out of the twenty-seven books of the New Testament (Paul's letters) were a result of the ministry that was launched in this historic moment of prayer and fasting.

So I think it is fair to say that God was pleased to make worship and prayer and fasting the launching pad for a mission that would change the course of world history. Is there a lesson here for us?[2]

Here, Piper is saying that the leadership of the early church at Antioch in Acts 13 had committed to give themselves to worship, prayer, and fasting, and it was from this posture of humility of heart that the Lord thrust them into the harvest fields. Furthermore, according to the broader testimony of the entire Book of Acts, prayer and missions have always gone hand in hand. It is only in the last few decades that we have separated the task of world evangelization from the labor of prayer and worship. Worship-fueled prayer and missions have always been two sides of the same coin. All truly effective Christian missions and ministry are birthed from the place of prayer and fasting and not just good planning and strategies.

Because finishing the task of world evangelization is the greatest task before us but also the hardest to achieve, only a mighty movement of prayer can topple the strongholds that hold people captive in the hardest and darkest places of the earth. Walter Wink says this: "History belongs to the intercessors, who believe the future into being. If this is so, then intercession, far from being an escape from action, is a means of focusing for action and of creating action. By means of our intercessions we veritably cast fire upon the earth and trumpet the future into being."[3]

Only aggressive and unified prayer will cause the giants of Islam, Hinduism, Buddhism, and every other ideology opposed to the Son of God to fall. For the last two thousand years all of heaven has waited with bated breath for the consummation of all things that will come only when the Son is exalted by every tribe, tongue, people, and nation. It is only through the worldwide program of prayer that the church will fulfill its calling as the community that possesses the revelation against whom the gates of hell will not prevail.

If we will understand prayer as God's invitation to us that allows us to change history, then we will not tinker around in our quiet times, prayer meetings, or church services. Instead, we will see our corporate times of prayer as the very battlefield where heaven and hell collide.

Think about this. Whenever God has wanted to establish His reign on the earth, He has first called His people to prayer, so we will never finish the task of the Great Commission without first being a praying people. The command of Jesus to preach the gospel in all nations was preceded by the command to pray: "Pray the Lord of the harvest to send out laborers" (Matt. 9:38). If this command of Jesus is true and worth obeying, then the task of finishing world evangelization in our lifetime is wholly dependent upon the prayers of His people. Thus, what God has brought together in prayer and mission, let no man tear asunder.

Since Jesus first gave His command to the church to go therefore and make disciples of all nations, there was always an end goal in His mind: a singing remnant taken from every tribe, tongue, people, and nation (Isa. 42:10–12; Rev 7:9). And missiologists tell us that perhaps for the first time in the history of the church, we are on the doorstep of fulfilling the Great Commission in our generation. However, there yet remains nearly seven thousand people groups, unreached and sometimes even unengaged, with the gospel.

Every believer has a responsibility to do their part to end "gospel poverty" in the nations of the earth. There is no greater social injustice than a lack of access to the gospel of Jesus Christ. Everyone deserves a chance to know Jesus and to join in the song of the Spirit and the bride, beckoning His return.

A SONG TO CLOSE THE TIMES

Too often worship is seen as the preview before the main event of the sermon in our church services, but this simply reveals our lack of knowledge and understanding regarding worship. Worship is nothing less than a key that unlocks heaven as Jesus goes forth to vanquish His enemies and deliver His people into the next age of partnership with Him. The worship and prayer movement in that day will not be considered something reserved for parachurch ministries and organizations but will instead be front and center as the church rediscovers its identity as the bride of Christ and the house of prayer for all nations (Rev. 22:17, 20).

God reveals His end-time plan through prophecy to raise up a global worship and prayer movement that will sing a new song initiating the second coming of Jesus. As the return of Jesus quickly approaches, the church in its identity as the bride of Christ will only increasingly lift its voice in worship and intercession as it cries out for the return of Jesus.

Isaiah 42 is one of the most remarkable prophecies in scripture that supports the church's end-time identity and the significance and power of song:

> Sing to the LORD a new song,
>> his praise from the end of the earth,
> you who go down to the sea, and all that fills it,
>> the coastlands and their inhabitants.
> Let the desert and its cities lift up their voice,
>> the villages that Kedar inhabits;
> let the habitants of Sela sing for joy,
>> let them shout from the top of the
>>> mountains.
> Let them give glory to the LORD,
>> and declare his praise in the coastlands.
> The LORD goes out like a mighty man,
>> like a man of war he stirs up his zeal;

he cries out, he shouts aloud,
he shows himself mighty against his foes.
—ISAIAH 42:10–13, ESV

The command to sing is one of the most oft-reported commands of God in all of Scripture. Throughout the Prophets and all throughout the New Testament on into the Book of Revelation, singing is a distinctive activity and response of the saints to the majesty and beauty of God. The Books of Isaiah and Revelation particularly show the prominent role of singing in the activity of the church, both in the generation in which the Lord returns as well as into the next age.

But why is singing so prominent throughout the Bible? Why is song, along with prayer and missions, so important in God's redemptive program? There are at least three reasons.

1. Singing is discipleship.

Many people relegate the theological significance of singing to the periphery of the life of the church. However, in his letters to the Ephesians and Colossians the apostle Paul makes clear that singing is central to understanding and obeying the words of Christ. He directs the followers of Jesus, saying:

> Let the word of Christ dwell in you richly in all wisdom, *teaching and admonishing one another in psalms and hymns and spiritual songs, singing with grace* in your hearts to the Lord.
> —COLOSSIANS 3:16, EMPHASIS ADDED

> And do not be drunk with wine, in which is dissipation; but be filled with the Spirit, *speaking to one another in psalms and hymns and spiritual songs, singing and making melody* in your heart to the Lord.
>
> —Ephesians 5:18–19, emphasis added

If allowing the Word of Christ to dwell inside of us richly is important, then singing and worshipping is central to our maturity in Christ. If being filled with the Spirit is important in our walk of faith, Paul leads us to conclude that singing and "making melody in our hearts to the Lord" is a primary means of our growth and progression in faith. Perhaps the dearth of the revelation of Jesus and the lack of the fear of the Lord in the church today is in no small part due to the lack of singing to God from the Scriptures.

2. Singing is unifying.

Singing, perhaps like nothing else, has the ability to unify a group of people more quickly than any other medium of communication. It has the effective ability to bring people into agreement in prayer and in worship. The power of corporate song is undeniable.

3. Singing is affective.

Lastly, singing touches the deep emotions of a person like very few other things can. When you sing, you can feel great joy, gratitude, empathy, sadness, and almost any other emotion. As we've explored previously, God desires that we encounter His deep emotions for us, and through singing to Him about Him, He often touches us at the affective (emotional) level. Some of my greatest personal encounters with God have flowed out of singing songs of worship or singing scriptures back to God; perhaps you can relate. This activity has a unique way of cutting through the cerebral part of ourselves and touching the human heart.

All that to say, the power of song in the identity and daily practice of the bride of Christ is vital in the unfolding of the end-times, and it is no accident that the Holy Spirit is emphasizing this activity in the earth. The prayer and worship movement across the globe is spreading. The expression and understanding of Christianity today involves a daily commitment and practice of prayer and worship. It is becoming a new normal in the body of Christ, and I am encouraged, as I believe it to be another sign of the times in our generation.

I would encourage all believers to commit to a greater level of participation in this movement of the Holy Spirit sweeping across the globe. Allow singing to become a daily expression of prayer and devotion in your life. Although it may seem odd, the Scriptures are clear that the identity of the church should and will be a singing church. This is because worship is the ultimate goal of missions and discipleship. All of our evangelistic endeavors are ultimately intended for the exaltation of Jesus. The nations of the earth are His promised inheritance, and the advancement of the gospel and the salvation of souls is undertaken primarily because Jesus is worthy and deserving to be worshipped and adored by all peoples.

John Piper eloquently explains the convergence of worship and missions:

> Missions is not the ultimate goal of the Church. Worship is. Missions exists because worship doesn't. Worship is ultimate, not missions, because God is ultimate, not man. When this age is over, and the countless millions of the redeemed fall on their faces before the throne of God, missions will be no more. It is a temporary necessity. But worship abides forever.
>
> Worship, therefore, is the fuel and goal of missions. It's the goal of missions because in missions we simply aim to bring the nations into the white-hot enjoyment of God's glory. The goal of missions is the gladness of the peoples in the greatness of God. "The LORD reigns; let the earth rejoice; let the many coastlands be glad!" (Ps 97:1). "Let the peoples praise thee, O God; let all the peoples praise thee! Let the nations be glad and sing for joy!" (Ps 67:3-4).
>
> But worship is also the fuel of missions. Passion for God in worship precedes the offer of God in preaching. You can't commend what you don't cherish. Missionaries will never call out, "Let the nations be glad!" if they cannot say from the heart, "I rejoice in the Lord....I will be glad and exult in thee, I will sing praise to your name, O Most High" (Ps. 104:34, 9:2). Missions begins and ends in worship.[4]

The worth of Jesus is the great and undisputed *why* behind the *what, how,* and *when* of our worship. Only a vision of His great worth will fuel the hearts of His followers to run this race with endurance, enabled by His grace to obey all of His commands with great joy. Only a vision of His worth will ignite His disciples to "go therefore into all nations" not out of dry-wrought obedience, but because of awestruck lovesickness. When we see Jesus, we understand that He deserves all glory, power, honor, and dominion. Our lives wasted in extravagant devotion and radical obedience are ultimately measured as a reasonable response to His matchless, eternal, immeasurable beauty. He deserves the nations as His inheritance because of who He is and because of what He has done. He deserves unceasing praise and worship from all people in every language.

WILL YOU GO?

We stand on the brink of the fulfillment of Matthew 24:14, where the gospel of the kingdom will have been proclaimed throughout the whole world as a testimony to all nations before the end of the age. While we look back over the history of gospel expansion, we are greatly indebted to men and women of previous generations who labored for the gospel to reach the ends of the earth.

However, even as we look back at history, we must remind ourselves that the task of world evangelization, though close to being complete, is still not done. The Joshua Project, a ministry that tracks gospel expansion among the final unreached and unengaged people groups of the earth, still lists nearly seven thousand people groups without a witness of the gospel.[5] There is still a great need in this generation for willing vessels—lovers of Jesus who will cast themselves wholeheartedly into the great task at hand. There is still time to dive into what God is doing in the earth. There is still a window for eternal and glorious impact available to this generation of believers.

I believe the apostle Paul, who gave himself to the work of missions like few others in his generation, would have been envious of these days. Paul made it his ambition to preach Christ where His name was not named, believing the words of Christ that once the unreached were reached, Jesus would return. Imagine how effective someone like the apostle Paul would be in our current missions landscape, given the ease of transportation and resources!

These are exciting days. And for those whose hearts burn to follow Jesus, obey His commands, and love Him wholeheartedly, the task of fulfilling the Great Commission has never been more attainable. It is not void of risk and hardship, of course. But following Jesus in even the most general sense was never promised to be void of risk or hardship. Though most people in the West, even Christians, flee suffering rather than take risks that bring about dangerous situations, risk is right. I would rather risk my life on the battlefront of missions than risk the loss of this unique opportunity before us to usher in the second coming of Jesus.

Even so, these final frontiers of modern missions are the most daunting. Only the most difficult regions are left to be reached. Only the hardest and darkest places remain, waiting for the great light of the gospel to penetrate them.

What kind of man and woman will it take to reach the final frontiers with the gospel of Jesus Christ? What sort of missionary must God produce in this generation to finish the task of world evangelization among the Muslim, Hindu, animistic, Buddhist, atheistic, and pagan people groups of the earth? The Scriptures are clear that in the last days the Lord is going to raise up a people who have overcome by the blood of the Lamb and the word of their testimony, and who will love not their own lives even unto death (Rev. 12:11).

As we look at our lives, can we say we love not our lives even unto death? Or is it truer that we shrink back in fear at the mere thought of persecution and suffering? When we look back over our lives fifty years from now, will we have been cut down while on the front lines of missions, daring to risk our very lives for the advancement of the gospel, or will we perish in our retirement and nursing homes with full bank accounts and successful portfolios, grasping at the last few straws of so-called comfort this life has to offer? With so much at stake, with so many souls in the balance, how can we continue with business as usual?

We, as Westerners, are so caught up in materialism and comfort that describing the Christian life as one of suffering seems foolish to us. But when will the gospel once again become what it once was—foolish, but dangerous? So few Christians choose risky and dangerous situations because so few want to choose suffering. However, this concept of self-preservation was foreign to the early church. Most of the teaching in our pulpits would probably seem alien to Paul, Peter, James, and John!

It comes down to what we value most: our own safety or His preeminent glory. Which is worth more to you? Who is Jesus to you, really? While persecution is foreign to almost every believer in the Western church, the Scriptures are clear that trials and persecutions should be expected by believers:

> Remember the word that I said to you, 'A servant is not greater than his master." If they persecuted Me, they will also persecute you.
>
> —John 15:20

> No one should be shaken by these afflictions; for you yourselves know that we are appointed to this. For, in fact, we told you before when we were with you that we would suffer tribulation, just as it happened, and you know.
>
> —1 Thessalonians 3:3–4

> We ourselves boast of you among the churches of God for your patience and faith in all your persecutions and tribulations that you endure, which is manifest evidence of the righteous judgment of God, that you may be counted worthy of the kingdom of God, for which you also suffer.
>
> —2 Thessalonians 1:4–5

> Yes, and all who desire to live godly in Christ Jesus will suffer persecution.
>
> —2 Timothy 3:12

> I now rejoice in my sufferings for you, and fill
> up in my flesh what is lacking in the afflictions
> of Christ, for the sake of His body, which is
> the church.
>
> —COLOSSIANS 1:24

> For to me, to live is Christ, and to die is gain.
>
> —PHILIPPIANS 1:21

Could "loving not our lives even unto death" mean that some of us, if not many of us, will have to give up our very lives to death before this is all over, for the sake of authentic love? What did Paul mean when he said that "all who desire to live godly in Christ Jesus will suffer persecution"? If the choices the apostles made that caused their suffering and even death seem so foreign to us, do we know what true apostolic Christianity is? Are we willing to give all, including our reputations and our lives, in order to gain Christ?

Perhaps we have been sold a lie that Christianity means never having to suffer another day. Perhaps we've been sold a lie that following Jesus is easy, comfortable, and safe. Something has to give in this generation to reverse the culture of easy believism, comfort, and convenience that would have been so unrecognizable to the early church, where they were more accustomed to trials, tribulations, persecutions, and martyrdom for the sake of the gospel.

Or perhaps you've been sold the lie that some places are closed to receiving the gospel—that going isn't an option even if you wanted to say yes. To that I say we should never agree or believe there is such a thing as a closed nation. Such a concept does not really exist. It only exists in our consciousness when the notion of suffering is something we cannot bear or understand.

The apostle Paul never would have accepted the notion that a nation or city (such as Lystra, Iconium, or Antioch) was closed off to him or the gospel simply because the people of that nation or city were hostile toward Christ. He was not concerned with maintaining the status quo of Western Christianity. He was not concerned with bodily comfort or upward mobility. Rather, his only concern was the glory of God being revealed to both Jews and Gentiles worldwide.

In his book *Last of the Giants* George Otis Jr. speaks to this, challenging the church to risk safety and to give itself to preaching the gospel where no one else has dared to go. He writes:

> The primary question being asked by would-be missionaries and mobilizers today is not, "Is the field ripe?" but, with increasing frequency, "Is it safe?" If relative freedom and safety cannot be affirmed satisfactorily, the only prudent option is to step back and wait for God to "open doors." But what is meant by the term open doors? By popular definition, the concept clearly involves more than mere assurance of personal safety. Opportunity and feasibility are cast as equally important components, demanding in the first case some kind of legitimatizing invitation or welcome to minister, and in the second

a realistic resources-to-challenge ratio. With either of these factors absent, the assumption is made that the doors to effective ministry are, for the time being, at least, "closed."

Despite the prevalence of such notions, a careful reexamination of the New Testament places them in clear conflict with the view and practices of the early Church. The idea, for instance, that God's servants must be welcomed in their ambassadorial roles is nowhere encountered. The record shows that from Jerusalem and Damascus to Ephesus and Rome, the apostles were beaten, stoned, conspired against and imprisoned for their witness. Invitations were rare, and never the basis for their missions....Spiritual inroads into enemy territory are nearly always the result of godly initiatives rather than heathen invitations. God's strategy in reclaiming His fallen creation is decidedly aggressive: Rather than wait for the captive souls to petition for liberation, He dispatches His servants instead on extensive search-and-rescue missions.[6]

I believe that understanding the cross of Jesus Christ and His demand that we take up our own crosses daily is the basis of our discipleship. When we see God as crucified, we understand He died not only to take away our sins, but also to show us how we could daily take up our own crosses. In other words, Jesus did not die on the cross only so we would not have to. He died on the cross to show us how we could.

We must recognize that God's purpose in suffering is actually fellowship. God is not a cruel master, and He does nothing without a purpose. In suffering, we experience fellowship with God as the one who, for the joy set before Him, endured the cross, committed Himself to obedience even to the point of death, and prevailed. Persecution, suffering, and martyrdom are not some morbid responses to Jesus but a glorious fellowship with Him that puts His eternal and matchless worth on display. Suffering and physical persecution are signs that we have sold all and that Jesus alone is enough for us. It's a way of proclaiming that nothing else can satisfy us, not even our physical health or emotional stability.

In light of the task at hand, the nations and people groups left to be reached with the good news of Jesus, and the suffering and likely persecution that must be endured in these particular regions to reach them, we need a change in our current Christian understanding. We must return to an understanding and expression of Christianity that reflects the simplicity and purity of the gospel message—that Jesus is Lord and worthy of all our love, even unto death. When this becomes our understanding and the prevailing witness of our lives, when the fear of suffering is overcome by lovesick abandon, we shall be virtually unstoppable as a force advancing the kingdom of God in the earth.

For my part, I was apprehended by the Lord just over five years ago with a vision to finish the task of world evangelization in this generation, and I have given myself wholeheartedly to this vision ever since. I believe it is possible in our generation to see the fulfillment of the command of Jesus that the gospel would be preached and disciples be made in every nation, people, and language. My faith has only increased as I see the convergence of the prayer and worship movement with the missions movement.

I believe the only way to finish the task to reach these hard and hostile regions of the earth is through the power of prayer and worship combined with the lovesick courage of willing vessels to "go therefore." The times we are living in are too wonderful. The opportunity to throw ourselves into what God is doing in this generation has never been so exciting. If this generation would refuse fear and lackadaisical living, if we would arise in faith and follow the Lamb wherever He goes, even to the hardest and darkest regions of the earth, surely He would arise "like a mighty man" and respond with wonders beyond what we could imagine, even His very return to this planet. Let us respond to the amazing opportunity in our lifetime, yes, even if it costs us our very lives.

REFLECTION QUESTIONS

John Piper famously declared that there are only three responses to the Great Commission for every believer: go, send, or disobey. What are you doing to fulfill the Great Commission through your life?

When was the last time you shared the gospel with someone? Have you shared the good news with your next door neighbors? If not, make a decision and set a time to share His message with your neighbor or someone in your life.

— — — — — — — — —

Father, You promised to give Jesus all the nations of the earth as His inheritance. You promised that out of every tribe, tongue, and people, worship and adoration for the name of Jesus would rise like incense. Thank You for inviting me into this story, for giving me permission to partner with You in what You are doing in the earth in my generation. Today I shake off the apathy that I've lived under for far too long, and I commit to obey Your commands as my response of love to You. I ask You to awaken me to Your heart's desires and purposes. Use me for Your glory, and send me as a witness of Your glorious gospel, even to the ends of the earth. Amen.

Chapter 9

FRIENDS OF THE BRIDEGROOM

He must increase, but I must decrease.

—JOHN 3:30

LOOKING PAST THE multitude that had gathered from miles around, you could make out his disheveled countenance. His hair in dreads, his beard long and thick, his clothing a crudely cut camel's hide, and his skin darkly tanned—evidence of many years spent out in this wilderness. But his voice was what arrested your attention, and his words are what gripped your heart.

It had been hundreds of years since Israel had received a true prophet of God. Generations had died out only hearing tales of this former glory, a time when God spoke through His messengers, holy men and women, set apart in their age. Then silence for four hundred years.

Now whispers of His Spirit's anointing had prevailed, and hope for the thunderings of His voice still rang true in the heart of Israel. Looking at John, the hope and hunger overflowed, and people poured out in droves to hear him speak.

His message was cutting, a call to repentance. It gave voice to the ache in the heart of God's people to return to the purity of obedience and devotion lost in the chaos of Roman occupation, corrupt leadership, and spiritual confusion.

The rumors of John's birth story fed the suspicions of many. "Could this be the hope of Israel?" they asked. "Could John be the Promised One we have been waiting for?"

After all, his father was a well-known rabbi, and the supernatural events leading to John's birth offered stark contrast to the lifeless spiritual landscape of the day. The angel Gabriel's appearance, Elizabeth's barren-ness healed, Zacharias's mute state for nine months that gave way to a landslide of speech that spoke the infant's name as John, a nonexistent name in the family line. Added to all this, John's parents saw fit to send him to this wilderness at such a young age to live set apart from the status quo, dedicated to God despite the blow to their reputation and livelihood.

Yes, John's life was remarkable in light of the spiritual climate of that day. And now that he'd begun to speak, the evidence of God's hand on his life was undeniable. His message cut to the core and gave voice to the ache of a generation: "Repent, for the kingdom of heaven is at hand!" (Matt. 3:2).

Yet John didn't jump at the chance for political or spiritual platform. Even when the spiritual leadership of the day—the Pharisees and Sadducees—came to him, he did not temper his message. John spoke with such clarity, conviction, and courage that his words still resonate their cutting power to this day. Brood of vipers, anyone?

But what is remembered about John the Baptist is not his thriving revival ministry. It's what Jesus said about him: "Truly I say to you, among those born of women there has not arisen anyone greater than John the Baptist!" (Matt. 11:11, NAS).

What about John elicited such a statement from Jesus? If we knew, surely we who also want to live set apart could learn to do the same. We receive much hope, then, when we consider what Jesus said next in His grand declaration of John: "Yet the one who is least in the kingdom of heaven is greater than he" (v. 11, NAS).

John's life was not meant to be an anomaly. His life is a prototype for those wanting to live consecrated to God. We can glean from the life of John the Baptist in our pursuit of wholehearted obedience and passion for Jesus.

One Who Pointed Toward the Light

John the Baptist did not lead an easy life by any means. He was truly set apart in his generation and walked in a unique authority as the forerunner to Jesus's first coming. His life had a clear, focused purpose, and he gave himself wholeheartedly to the call of God on his life. Yet the significance of his life is measured not in ministry stats but in his heart response. You see, even though John was described as a burning and shining torch (John 5:35) and the greatest man born of a woman (Matt. 11:11), he did not identify himself that way. On the contrary, his heart was founded in a place of such security before God that there was a remarkable lack of selfish ambition, competition, and self-seeking in him.

For four hundred years no one talked like this man. He spoke with the authority of a prophet, causing thousands to flock to him in the middle of an unforgiving desert. He had become a bright star in the midst of a dark night in Israel's history. He restored faith to a people who had almost lost all hope. He and his disciples were swept into a mighty torrent of awakening, shaping the future of their people.

But just as quickly as his star rocketed into the sky, it was washed out when a more brilliant light, the bright Morning Star, burned before the people. John's disciples could not understand it, and envy crept into their hearts, eating away at their newfound purpose and meaning in life. They didn't realize that in the coming of Jesus, John's joy was now complete, his greatest desire now fulfilled. We see it clearly in John 3:

> Therefore there arose a discussion on the part of John's disciples with a Jew about purification. And they came to John and said to him, "Rabbi, He who was with you beyond the Jordan, to whom you have testified, behold, He

is baptizing and all are coming to Him." John answered and said, "A man can receive nothing unless it has been given him from heaven. You yourselves are my witnesses that I said, 'I am not the Christ,' but, 'I have been sent ahead of Him.' He who has the bride is the bridegroom; but the friend of the bridegroom, who stands and hears him, rejoices greatly because of the bridegroom's voice. So this joy of mine has been made full. He must increase, but I must decrease."

—JOHN 3:25–30, NAS

John describes himself as a friend of the Bridegroom and points everyone to the superior glory and beauty of Jesus. He doesn't do this because this is the humble thing to do. He is genuinely full of joy in this declaration! The sincere and primary goal and passion of John's heart was to prepare the way, to ready men's hearts to receive Jesus. John demonstrated a life of courageous abandon to the things of God, and it provoked his generation to reach for God.

The truth is, John never set out to be a radical public figure. He never made it his aim to become great in the eyes of men. John's primary ambition was to make much of Jesus. He was content to be a forerunner, a precursor, the opening band to the real headliner. When confronted with the loss of ministry advancement as the crowds and even many of his own disciples left to follow Jesus, John's true motives were brought to light. He said, "I am not the Christ, but I have been sent ahead of Him."

John's ministry and life reveal to us that we are not the point of life. Only Jesus is. John understood that this is God's story. We are not the hero of the story. We are not the Savior. The single greatest blow to the pride in every human heart is that it's not about us. It was always, is always, and will always be about Him.

HEARTS THAT STEAL GOD'S GLORY

I remember a time when I felt this become real in my own life. I was in my early twenties at the time and preaching at a youth conference. I felt remarkably weak in my capacity to impart anything to the conference attendees. They were mostly high school age, and if you've ever preached to high schoolers, you understand they can be a tough crowd. I just pressed through my message, feeling absolutely nothing, not an ounce of Holy Spirit activity in a tangible way. I walked off the stage feeling totally dejected, a little embarrassed, and just grateful to be done. I remained in my seat while the ministry time continued, and I started dialoguing with God.

As I was praying, I heard the Holy Spirit whisper to my spirit so clearly I'll never forget it. He said, "Brian, for the first time it wasn't about you. Thank you for giving Me friends."

I crumbled in that moment, weeping as I felt God's kindness. I had been operating out of so much performance, looking for man's opinion as my litmus test of success or failure, that I had made the platform more about me than I realized. And God used that moment when I felt so weak and unanointed to correct me in His gentle way.

God is so much more interested in His glory than our personal comfort and success. He will tirelessly confront the pride and self-seeking motives within us because He is committed to the bigger picture: the eternal exaltation of Jesus as Lord of all. When we fix our eyes on that higher vision, selfish ambition fades, loneliness is redeemed, and joyful expectation becomes our portion.

But this is not how we often live.

By way of illustration, just imagine for a moment that you are at a wedding. The bride is about to enter the scene. Everyone can sense the groom's excitement. The air is thick with anticipation. So much care and planning has gone into this day and into this moment. The music begins to crescendo. The officiant motions for all to rise in honor of the bride. This is her moment.

The doors open and a gasp of admiration erupts in the sanctuary. The bride steps forward, her father at her side. She has waited her whole life for this moment. She is breathtaking, a vision in white and...

"Hey! Hey, guys! Hey, everyone!"

What? What's going on?

"Hey, guys! I'm over here! Everyone, look at me!"

Confused, people start to look around, whispering to each other in disbelief at this disruption.

"Everyone! I'm right here! Look at me!"

There in the midst of the congregation, a man is waving his hands. He's standing up on his pew, drawing all the attention to himself.

The sacred moment is lost. The bride's moment has been stolen.

Now, I realize this is a rather outrageous scenario, and yet, in essence, this happens every single day within the body of Christ. Each one of us is guilty of the same thoughtless action, the same inappropriate behavior and attitude. We are guilty of living our lives as if the moment is all about us when it's not. Whether we perceive this is what we're doing or not, so much of what we do and say is rooted in deep pride and selfish ambition. We live as heroes within our own imaginations, pop stars in our own little worlds.

This sentiment is not unique. It has existed within the hearts of men since that fateful moment when the forbidden fruit was bitten—even further still, before the creation of human beings, back when Satan was still an angel.

To demonstrate what I mean, I'll tell you about a conversation I shared with my two oldest children. They were six and four at the time. We were driving in the car, and my son brought up the topic of Satan, how he used to be an angel. My daughter, Evangeline, immediately asked, "Why did he stop being an angel?"

I told her it was because he saw how beautiful God was and got so jealous of God's beauty that he wanted to be more beautiful than God and for everyone else to love him instead of God.

My sweet girl then said, "Oh! I would *never* do that. Why did he do that?"

My son, in typical firstborn fashion, was quick to chime in, though, saying, "Oh, yes, you *would* do that, Eva, because you have *sin!*"

I laughed and quickly jumped in before this turned into an argument. "Well, Eva, I love that you don't want to do what Satan did, but I need you to know something. The same yuckiness that was in Satan when he wanted to be better than God is in our hearts too. It's called sin. And only Jesus can take that yuckiness and wash it away."

"But why is God the most beautiful?" she asked. "Why can't *we* be the most beautiful?"

I was stunned by her bluntness, cushioned by the sweet, innocent inquisitiveness of her four-year-old heart. I ceased to be the teacher in that moment, as the lesson I was so masterfully imparting struck my own heart in a new way.

"Well, Evangeline," I said, "He...just...*is*." I bumbled to find the right words. "He's the one who made beauty in the first place. He's the *most* beautiful one. But you know what? He isn't mean about it. He's so nice, so good and wonderful, that He actually shares His beauty with us."

Well, as most conversations with a four-year-old might progress, the topic changed and my daughter interrupted me to talk of princesses, wedding dresses, and other beautiful things in general while my son rolled his eyes and my heart kept pondering what had just happened.

Forgive my simplistic wording here, but what so struck my heart in talking with my four- and six-year-old kids is the part about the story being all about God but that somehow, in the fathomless goodness of God's heart, He has invited you and me into it. He has given us a glorious invitation and has written our names right into the main plotline. He has invited us into the adventure, into the discovery of His glory and the thrill of purpose and impact that our hearts so crave.

But we must not forget whose hand holds the pen and whose story this is ultimately all about. Paul stunningly describes the story line:

> For He rescued us from the domain of darkness, and transferred us to the kingdom of His beloved Son, in whom we have redemption, the forgiveness of sins.
>
> He is the image of the invisible God, the firstborn of all creation. For by Him all things were created, both in the heavens and on earth, visible and invisible, whether thrones or dominions or rulers or authorities—all things have been created through Him and for Him. He is before all things, and in Him all things hold together. He is also head of the body, the church; and He is the beginning, the firstborn from the dead, so that He Himself will come to have first place in everything. For it was the Father's good pleasure for all the fullness to dwell in Him, and through Him to reconcile all things to Himself, having made peace through the blood of His cross; through Him, I say, whether things on earth or things in heaven.
>
> —COLOSSIANS 1:13–20, NAS

In the end Christ will be found preeminent in all things. He shall be exalted to the highest place. He is the Bridegroom. The bride belongs to Him. Whatever our pursuits, whatever our motivations, they must flow out of a right understanding of Christ's preeminence.

This is what it looks like to walk in the fear of the Lord. The fear of the Lord is a right perspective of His supremacy. It is a right perspective of our place and His. When we walk in this right perspective, we walk in humility, just as John the Baptist did. When the fear of the Lord abides in your heart, when you see Him rightly, as the one who has the bride, the one who is in control, the one who is truly worthy, you are filled with joy and peace. Your identity crisis is resolved because you realize it's not your job to be the hero. You are not the answer to the world's problems. Jesus is. He has all the wisdom. He has all the power. He has all the beauty.

A Joy Fulfilled

In my experience every twenty-year-old thinks the world revolves around him or her, and it's not something you can just shake them out of. It takes time. It takes pruning, rebuking, and, like John, years spent in a wilderness. John's level of humility was not something he just came out of the womb possessing. He was just as human as you and I are. Humility was forged in his heart through years spent in the wilderness where he learned to hear the voice of God, came to believe his identity was sure before heaven, chose a lifestyle of extravagant devotion, and courageously obeyed the call of God on his life by trumpeting a call of repentance to a lost people.

John did not seek to be great before men. He sought out the one whose greatness is unsearchable, and he was set on fire by that search. John had a magnificent obsession, and it overpowered his pride and ambition. He was a burning and shining lamp not because he burned before the people but because he stood before the burning One and was set ablaze with holy passion.

Furthermore, John said his joy was fulfilled through the hearing of the Bridegroom's voice:

> But the friend of the bridegroom, who stands and hears him, rejoices greatly because of the bridegroom's voice. Therefore this joy of mine is fulfilled. He must increase, but I must decrease."
> —John 3:29–30

A treasure of intimacy with God is found in this right place of humility. When we are quiet, when our strife is stilled, we hear His voice—the same voice that spoke the universe into existence. When we hear Him, our hearts burn within us as He speaks. The prophet Jeremiah put it this way: "Your words were found, and I ate them, and Your word was to me the joy and rejoicing of my heart; for I am called by Your name, O LORD God of hosts" (Jer. 15:16). The disciples who walked with Jesus on the road to Emmaus after His resurrection put it this way: "Did not our heart burn within us while He talked with us on the road, and while He opened the Scriptures to us?" (Luke 24:32).

There is a joy in hearing the voice of God that is more real than we know. The joy of intimacy with God—to talk with Him, to commune with Him in fellowship and love—is what the human heart was created for.

Your heart longs to make impact in the world. You long to put your hand to something of eternal significance. Then go to Him. Hear Him. He'll set you on fire. Let Him give you a real message. I'm not talking about a good sermon or a tweetable nugget. I'm speaking of the reality of becoming so obsessed, so on fire for the glory of God that *you become a message.* Your life becomes a living witness of the beauty of Jesus Christ, the risen and returning Lord of all.

There is a place in friendship with Jesus that is beyond all semblance of strife. The sweetness and surpassing joy of intimacy becomes more than an ideal. It becomes real. When you are a friend of God, He invites you into a place of partnership with His heart. He shares His secrets with those who walk in the fear of the Lord (Ps. 25:14). He invites us into a glorious partnership with the Holy Spirit's agenda in the earth to glorify Jesus as supreme above all—not partnership on a merely cerebral level or in verbiage alone, but partnership in every arena of life.

He invites you not just to raise a torch, but to *be* a torch. Burning, blazing, like beacons in the night pointing the weary traveler to their destination. He fills His friends with His Spirit, and like John, He gives them a message of hope for a lost people, the message that He is coming.

A GENERATION OF FORERUNNERS

Behold, I will send you Elijah the prophet before
the great and awesome day of the LORD comes.
—MALACHI 4:5, ESV

I believe that as we stand on the precipice of the second
coming of Jesus, the Lord is raising up an entire generation of forerunners who are walking in the same
spirit of Elijah that John walked in to prepare the way
of the Lord. They will be a company of fiery passionate
believers. And they, like John, will carry a consuming
obsession with the beauty and greatness of Jesus and
spend their lives as bright messengers of His glory. Like
John, their lives will not be marked by the amount of
comfort and favor they attain, but rather by the joyful
humility they carry as they walk out obedience to the
call of God on their lives and His ultimate purposes in
the earth.

Malachi prophesied that the spirit of Elijah would
preempt the coming of the Lord. The angel Gabriel referenced this prophecy when he spoke of John the Baptist
to his father Zachariah (Luke 1:17). This spirit of Elijah
that rested on John to prepare the way of Jesus's first
coming will also be poured out upon the generation pre-
ceding the second coming of Jesus.

The "great and awesome day of the Lord" is coming,
and there will come a day when real men's hearts will
faint from fear. There will come a day when the church
everywhere is persecuted and the faith of every believer
is refined. There will come a day when a real Antichrist

will sit in Jerusalem and demand that all men worship him. But ultimately, there will come a day when Jesus, our King, Savior, and Bridegroom, will split the sky and return to this planet.

The end-times are not a list of imaginary or symbolic events. They are real. And whatever your theological views on the subject, whether you agree with my particular eschatology or not, I think we can agree that the Bible is clear in this matter: to be a disciple of Jesus is to live in hopeful expectation of His soon return.

Early Christianity was never about dying and going to heaven. It was about being faithful to the commands of Jesus until death while fully expecting and believing that Jesus would return soon, as He had promised. The first Christians were given in the work of evangelism, discipleship, and church planting. Enduring persecution and martyrdom, they pressed on in their goal to preach the gospel to the ends of the earth. Why? Because then the end would come.

The apostle Paul made it his aim to preach Christ where His name was not named. His entire life was given to this cause of partnering with the Holy Spirit to accomplish the work of maturing the bride, furthering the spread of the gospel to all the earth, and remaining personally faithful in love to Jesus. His primary motivation was love. It compelled him in all his endeavors. He believed Jesus would return when the task was finished, and this hope fueled his efforts.

The longing for Christ's return is a marked distinctive of His followers. After all, when you love someone and they are not with you, you miss them. You mourn their absence and wait with anticipation to be reunited. Until Jesus, the one whom our soul loves, returns to Earth, we miss Him. We ache for Him. And through lifestyles of mourning for the Bridegroom (Matt. 9:15) we shine a message of eternal hope to a desperate world.

Until Jesus returns, things are not as they should be. But He promised He would come back, and when He comes back, He's going to make all the wrongs things right. He is going to take His place as the King this earth so desperately needs, the judge the world is groaning for, and the Bridegroom every human heart was created to love and be loved by.

He is coming back. Your life should scream that reality. You heart should burn for this truth. *He is coming back.* This should disrupt you. This should excite you. This should make you tremble with holy fear and inexpressible joy. There is more promised to us in our Christian experience than just the fact that when we die we'll be spared from hell and get to live in heaven, although that is pretty awesome.

We have hope that Jesus will return, and when He does, He will redeem every single moment of this earthly existence by taking His rightful place on a real throne in a real city and ruling in righteousness, in partnership with His faithful remnant as a reward for their faith and love. This hope is more sufficient and all-consuming than just the hope of going to heaven. Why? Because it's about Him, not you. His return is not only about vindicating your faith. His return is also about His glory.

When your hope rests fully in the reality that this is ultimately His story, your heart is released from striving. You are given the invitation to get caught up in His story, something bigger than yourself, exceeding anything you could conceive or imagine for your own life. If this becomes the reality of your heart before God, a thousand issues are settled. *What is God's will for my life? What should my career path be? What nation should I go be a missionary to? Whom should I marry? I'm not happy in my life—what's missing? Does this person like me? Why is my ministry not growing?* Living in the fear of the Lord and in the hope of His return settles so many issues. Life makes sense when we keep the return of Jesus in perspective. We live with urgency and purpose, but also with a deep inner peace in the knowledge that He will perfect the good work He began. He will receive the reward of His suffering and be glorified as Lord of all, high and lifted up.

THE CALL TO A DECREASING LIFE

In the Western world we find ourselves swept into a current of upward mobility. The sentiment and drive of our culture teaches us that we must move up in life, climbing the ladder and making it to the top, that success and promotion, wealth, and white fences are the key to happiness. We are taught from birth that we must pursue more, always going after what's bigger and better. Even within the church this sentiment prevails. A clawing for platform and a drive for promotion exists.

But true joy is not found in upward mobility. The human heart was not made to find contentment in the increase but rather in the decrease. Henri Nouwen explains this concept in his book *The Selfless Way of Christ*:

> If anything is certain, it is that this nation desires to be the best, the strongest, and the most powerful. The attitude of "We're number one!" is nurtured with all diligence and on all levels: in athletics, business, technology and military power...
>
> The story of our salvation stands radically over and against the philosophy of upward mobility. The great paradox which Scripture reveals to us is that real and total freedom is only found through downward mobility. The Word of God came down to us and lived among us as a slave. *The divine way is indeed the downward way.*[1]

When we consider Jesus, the one whom we love, the one whom we forsake all else to follow, we see a very different path. We see an example of humility so blatantly opposed to the sentiments of our culture, it might as well be black and white. We behold one who was before time, dwelling in glory with the Father, becoming a small, helpless infant, living a life of obscurity and hiddenness, despised and rejected, having no beauty that we should desire Him. We see not the glory of a rising star but the beauty of an emptied life. Jesus demonstrated that the way of God is not grasping for more but becoming low, empty, and humble:

Have this attitude in yourselves which was also in Christ Jesus, who, although He existed in the form of God, did not regard equality with God a thing to be grasped, but emptied Himself, taking the form of a bond-servant, and being made in the likeness of men. Being found in appearance as a man, He humbled Himself by becoming obedient to the point of death, even death on a cross.

—Philippians 2:5–8, nas

Jesus makes it clear that the way He lived is the pathway we should follow. Again and again He emphasized the downward way, but not without promise of great reward. There is joy in the letting go. Such sweet fellowship with Christ is experienced in the surrender.

When John the Baptist spoke of this joy, he described it as being fulfilled. He experienced full, satisfying joy when He heard the Bridegroom's voice, and it spurred a cry within him for even more of this emptying, even more of this decreased life. As he famously said, "He must increase, but I must decrease" (John 3:30). When we are emptied, He may fill us with all the fullness of His Spirit.

Christ is not a supplement. He's not an additional bullet point in our personal agenda. He's not a sideshow. He is all in all. His rightful place is at the center of our hearts as Lord. As we taste of Him, as we behold Him, we are transformed. Our cry ceases to be a self-focused appeal for satisfaction. We become consumed with a cry for the increase of Christ, the increase of His kingdom, the increase of His glory in the earth and within our hearts.

A FINAL APPEAL

When you think of great men and women of faith who were burning and shining lamps in their generation, who comes to mind? I think of such people as Amy Carmichael and Hudson Taylor. I think of missionaries who left everything behind to bring the gospel to the unreached regions of the earth. I think of Paul the Apostle, Stephen the Martyr, John the Beloved, and Mary of Bethany. I think of Billy Graham, Heidi Baker, Mike Bickle, Lou Engle, Dick Eastman, and other men and women serving the Lord in closed nations today, people whose names I can't even mention for risk of their lives.

But those great men and women of the faith remembered in history books and esteemed in later generations never made it their aim to be remembered in history books. On the contrary, they were the "great forgotten" of their generations. Willing to bear the loneliness, rejection, and ill-repute of lives lived in the crucible of misunderstood devotion, they were willing to be completely forgotten, sowing their lives instead upon the soil of eternal hope and building a memorial of heavenly remembrance. Resurrection is never experienced before the death and burial. Their lives testify that a surrendered life is the most liberated; a crucified life is the most alive.

Are you willing to follow in their footsteps by following this beautiful Man? Are you willing to pursue the knowledge of God with your whole heart, to abandon the pursuit of lesser things and allow your heart to become consumed with the inexpressible joy of fascination of Jesus? There is no promise of ease, but there is promise of great reward. There is no promise of increase, but there is a promise of decrease that magnifies His name and draws you closer and closer to Him, the Source of all life. This was the secret John the Baptist knew. You will experience moments of loneliness. You will face trials of many kind. Those are true expectations. But you'll also experience peace that surpasses knowledge, uncontainable joy, exhilarating freedom, and deep, incomparable satisfaction.

Jesus is a grand adventure. He is a good author, and this story He is writing is beyond what you can conceive or imagine for your own life. Surrender to Him. Choose His way. Though it is the way of the cross, it leads to life.

Consider the appeal of Charles Spurgeon in his famed sermon on being a friend of God:

> To be friends, *we must exercise a mutual choice*— the God who has chosen you must be chosen by you. Most deliberately, heartily, resolutely and undividedly you must choose God to be your God and your Friend. Beloved, there can be no friendship between you and God without your own full consent, nor without your ardent desire. What do you say to this? If sin is pardoned, all ground of enmity is gone—but now Grace must come in to reign through righteousness unto eternal life—and bring you into

a condition of tender love and fervent desire towards the Lord our God.

But even then you have not gone far enough. If we are to be the friends of God, there must be a *conformity of heart*, will, design and character to God. Can two walk together except they are agreed? Will God accept as His friend one who despises holiness, who is careless in obedience, who has no interest in the purposes of Divine Love, no delight in the Gospel of Christ? Beloved, the Holy Spirit must make us like God or else we cannot be friends of God! We must love Jesus the Son, or we cannot love the Father! We cannot rise to the standard of friends of God if self is our ruling force. God is not selfish and He is not the friend of the selfish. Unless we love what God loves and hate what God hates, we cannot be His friends. Our lives must, in the main, run in parallel lines with the life of the gracious, holy and loving God, or else we shall be walking contrary to Him and He will walk contrary to us.

If we have got as far as that, then the next thing will surely follow—there must be a *continual communion*. The friend of God must not spend a day without God and he must undertake no work apart from his God. Oh, to live *with* God and *in* God and *for* God and *like* God! You cannot be a friend of God if your communion with Him is occasional, fitful, distant, broken. If you only think of Him on Sundays or at sacraments, you cannot be His friend! Friends love each other's society—the friend of God must abide in God, walk with God—and then he shall dwell at ease. What do you say to this? Has the Grace of God made your feet like hinds' feet to stand on such high places? He can do it. Let us seek after the blessing.[2]

May your life be marked by friendship with God. May you join with those of us whose lives are marked by the most magnificent obsession of all.

REFLECTION QUESTIONS

John the Baptist was a man on fire. Jesus said of him that he was a burning and shining lamp and that his generation was willing to rejoice in his light for a short time. In what ways is your heart burning for Jesus and shining His light to those around you?

This book has been about a magnificent obsession—namely, a fascination with Jesus that consumes our very lives. In what ways has your obsession with Jesus grown as you've journeyed through this conversation?

— — — — — — — —

Jesus, author and finisher of my faith, I thank You for inviting me into the grand story You are writing. I thank You that I can trust Your perfect leadership in my life as You orchestrate all things for Your glory. I ask that You would consume me with a vision of Your matchless worth. I long to be Your friend in this hour of history, to know the fulfilling joy of hearing Your voice and partnering with Your heart. I long to follow You in wholehearted love and burn with passion for You all my days. Make me a friend of the Bridegroom, walking in the same humility, fear of the Lord, and selfless love that John the Baptist walked in. Let my life shine as a burning testament of Your glory in the earth until You split the sky and take Your rightful place as the King of the whole earth and desire of all nations. I long for Your return, and together with Your Spirit I cry, "Come, Lord Jesus." Amen.

Appendix A

RECOMMENDING READING BY CHAPTER

CHAPTER 1
THE MOST IMPORTANT QUESTION

Bickle, Mike. *Jesus: Our Magnificent Obsession, Part 1* and *Jesus: Our Magnificent Obsession, Part 2*. Free teaching series available at http://mikebickle.org/resources/series/jesus-our-magnificent-obsession and http://mikebickle.org/resources/series/jesus-our-magnificent-obsession-part-2.

Charnock, Stephen. *The Existence and Attributes of God*. Grand Rapids, MI: Baker Books, 1996.

Tozer, A. W. *Knowledge of the Holy*. New York: HarperCollins, 1961.

Chapter 2
A Life of One Thing

Bickle, Mike. *Growing in Prayer: A Real-Life Guide to Talking With God*. Lake Mary, FL: Charisma House, 2014.

Dubay, Thomas. *Fire Within*. San Francisco: Ignatius Press, 1989.

Nouwen, Henri. *Clowning in Rome*. New York: Doubleday Books, 1979.

_____. *The Way of the Heart*. New York: Ballantine, 2003.

Sorge, Bob. *Secrets of the Secret Place*. Grandview, MO: Oasis House, 2001.

Chapter 3
The God Who Responds

Chan, Francis. *Crazy Love*. Colorado Springs, CO: David C. Cook, 2008.

Manning, Brennan. *The Furious Longing of God*. Colorado Springs, CO: David C. Cook, 2009.

_____. *The Relentless Tenderness of Jesus*. Grand Rapids, MI: Revell, 2004.

Chapter 4
An Extravagant Devotion

Bickle, Mike. *Passion for Jesus: Cultivating Extravagant Love for God*. Lake Mary, FL: Charisma House, 2007.

MacDonald, William. *True Discipleship*. Port Colborne, Ontario: Gospel Folio Press, 2003.

Platt, David. *Radical: Taking Back Your Faith From the American Dream*. Colorado Springs, CO: Multnomah, 2010.

CHAPTER 5
THE ANCIENT DREAM

Ravenhill, Leonard. *Revival Praying*. Bloomington, MN: Bethany House, 2005.

_____. *Why Revival Tarries*. Bloomington, MN: Bethany House, 1987.

CHAPTER 6
OUR GREAT HELPER

I find the greatest encouragement by gleaning from real men and women who walked in deep encounter and friendship with the Holy Spirit. These books describe ordinary people who learned to rely on the Holy Spirit, listen to His voice, and obey His commands.

Brother Yun. *The Heavenly Man*. London: Monarch Books, 2002.

Cunningham, Loren. *Is That Really You, God?* Seattle: YWAM Publishing, 2001.

Eastman, Dick. *The Purple Pig and Other Miracles*. Lake Mary, FL: Charisma House, 2011.

Pullinger, Jackie. *Chasing the Dragon*. Ventura, CA: Regal Books, 1980.

Chapter 7
A Happy Holiness

Engle, Lou. *Nazirite DNA*. Audiobook available as a free download at http://thecall.com/Articles/1000104274/TheCall/Free/Nazirite_DNA.aspx.

Piper, John. *The Dangerous Duty of Delight*. Colorado Springs, CO: Multnomah, 2011.

Sorge, Bob. *A Covenant With My Eyes*. Grandview, MO: Oasis House, 2013.

Chapter 8
Singing Back the King

Nouwen, Henri. *The Selfless Way of Christ: Downward Mobility and the Spiritual Life*. Maryknoll, NY: Orbis Books, 2007.

Sorge, Bob. *It's Not Business, It's Personal*. Grandview, MO: Oasis House, 2009.

Chapter 9
Friends of the Bridegroom

Piper, John. *Let the Nations Be Glad: The Supremacy of God in Missions*. Grand Rapids, MI: Baker Academic, 2010.

Ripken, Nik. *The Insanity of God: A True Story of Faith Resurrected*. Nashville: B&H, 2013.

THE ANTIOCH CENTER FOR
TRAINING AND SENDING

"What if we were to finish the Great Commission in our generation?"

We believe that this generation can finish the task of reaching every unreached people group in the planet with the gospel. We know that this is an ambitious goal, but it is not an impossible goal. Through the leadership of the Holy Spirit, prayer, and the relentless and united effort of the church, we believe that the task of reaching every tribe, tongue, people, and nation with the gospel is courageously achievable.

The Antioch Center for Training and Sending (ACTS) is a missional community and movement based out of Colorado Springs, Colorado, that exists to equip and send ten thousand young pioneering leaders to finish the task of world evangelization, make disciples, and sing back the King.

We believe that God is building a new student volunteer movement with the potential to finish the task of world evangelization in this generation. Recognizing that this daring ambition will not be completed until the gospel of the kingdom is proclaimed to every tribe, tongue, people, and nation, we have prioritized the 10/40 Window as our field of action. According to the Joshua Project, of the world's sixteen thousand-plus people groups, nearly seven thousand are still unreached with the gospel of the kingdom. However, the Bible is clear that the gospel of the kingdom must be proclaimed to every people group of the earth before Jesus will return to establish His kingdom forever. To that end, our ambition is to equip and send young leaders to plant gospel-centered, presence-fueled, prayer furnaces/praying churches among the unreached and least-reached peoples of the world. For more information on how you can be equipped and join the movement to finish the task of world evangelization in this generation, please visit our school website: ACTSschool.com.

Appendix B

HOW TO STUDY THE BIBLE

PREPARE

Get vision

> Be diligent to present yourself approved to God, a worker who does not need to be ashamed, *rightly dividing the word of truth.*
> —2 TIMOTHY 2:15, EMPHASIS ADDED

> Now a certain Jew named Apollos...an eloquent man and *mighty in the Scriptures...*
> —ACTS 18:24, EMPHASIS ADDED

> All Scripture is given by *inspiration of God*, and is *profitable* for doctrine, for reproof, for correction, for instruction in righteousness, *that the man of God may be complete, thoroughly equipped for every good work.*
> —2 TIMOTHY 3:16-17, EMPHASIS ADDED

> For the word of God is *living* and *powerful*, and *sharper than any two-edged sword*, piercing even to the division of soul and spirit, and of joints and marrow, and is a *discerner of the thoughts and intents of the heart.*
>
> —HEBREWS 4:12, EMPHASIS ADDED

> "The words that I speak to you are spirit, and *they are life.*"...But Simon Peter answered Him, "Lord, to whom shall we go? You have the words of *eternal life.*"
>
> —JOHN 6:63, 68, EMPHASIS ADDED

Approach God

When we approach the Bible, we are approaching God Himself. In His infinite wisdom the Lord has determined to reveal Himself through the Scriptures. Thus, the Bible is not a mere historical curiosity or like any other book. The words are alive and powerful because they testify of Jesus, yet so few of us actually encounter the living God through His words of life. While the Scripture is objectively powerful, its purpose is to cause us to encounter Jesus.

> You search the Scriptures, for in them you think you have eternal life; and these are they which testify of Me. But you are not willing to *come to Me* that you may have life.
>
> —JOHN 5:39–40, EMPHASIS ADDED

Open your eyes

When I struggle to read through the Scripture, I pray the prayer of Psalm 119:18–20. The Lord will graciously empower you to not only endure the Scriptures, but also to love and desire His Word at all times.

> Open my eyes, that I may see
> Wondrous things from Your law.
> I am a stranger in the earth;
> Do not hide your commandments from me.
> My soul breaks with longing
> For Your judgments at all times.

READ WITH GOALS IN MIND

Breadth

Get a bird's-eye, big-picture perspective on the Bible. Read ten chapters per day, and read from both the Old Testament and the New Testament each day.

> For I have not shunned to declare to you *the whole counsel of God*.
> —ACTS 20:27, EMPHASIS ADDED

Depth

The Bible is as deep as it is wide. Oftentimes when we only focus on getting through our Bible plan, we miss the opportunity to encounter God in the depth of His Word.

Encounter and obedience

Again, the purpose of reading the Word is to know—encounter—God and obey His words. The spiritual disciplines are not an end in themselves but are means to the end of encountering and glorifying God in and through our lives.

KNOW THE APPROACHES

There are generally two approaches taken to Bible study. An inductive approach attempts to let conclusions evolve from observation, while a deductive approach comes to the text with a preconceived thesis with a view to let Scripture support that thesis. Here we'll look at an inductive approach to Bible study.

Observation

What does the text immediately say? Consider the who, what, when, where, why, and how, as well as the grammar, structure, context, occasion, and purpose. Be sure to write down in a journal things you do not understand initially from observation. Look for repeated words, themes, and key words. Pay attention to verb tenses, as well as moods and emotions described or implied.

Interpretation

What did the text mean when it was written? Continually ask *why* questions:

- Why did the author write this?

- Why did the hearers need to hear this?

- Why is a particular word continually repeated?

Genre often matters when interpreting Scripture. For more on literary genre and how to interpret Scripture in light of genre, see *How to Read the Bible for All Its Worth* by Gordon Fee and Douglas Stuart.

Historical background is also key when interpreting Scripture. We can understand historical background through internal evidence (what's found inside the text) as well as external evidence (what we know from sources outside the text).

INTERNAL EVIDENCE	EXTERNAL EVIDENCE
In the book itself	Bible dictionary/ encyclopedia
In other books of the Bible	Maps
	Books about customs and cultures
	Commentaries (consult these last)

Application

> But be doers of the word, and not hearers only, deceiving yourselves. For if anyone is a hearer of the word and not a doer, he is like a man observing his natural face in a mirror; for he observes himself, goes away, and immediately forgets what kind of man he was. But he who looks into the perfect law of liberty and continues in it, and is not a forgetful hearer but a doer of the work, this one will be blessed in what he does.
>
> —JAMES 1:22–25

This is where we ask, "How does the text apply to me today?" The quality of our application will depend upon the quality and time we spent on observation and interpretation of the text.

When we look for application in the text, we are searching for timeless truths that move us toward obedience to God. This step must begin in prayer, as the Holy Spirit convicts us of sin, righteousness, and judgment.

Some application questions we can ask include:

- What is the main, timeless truth in this text?

- In light of the truth(s) communicated in this text, what changes must I make in my life?

- How will I make these changes to obey the truth of God's Word? Be specific.

BRIDGE THE GAPS

Language

Obviously the Bible was not written in English, but in Greek, Hebrew, and Aramaic. While some of us may have been adequately trained to handle the original languages that the Scriptures were written in, that number of people is still very small.

Yet oftentimes understanding the meaning of a certain text in Scripture requires knowledge or understanding of the meaning of the word in the original language. There are many free tools online that can help you understand the original languages.

Culture

Even more difficult than understanding the original languages is the attempt to understand the culture in which the Bible was written and addressed. Without an understanding of Jewish culture, as well as the Greek and Roman cultures, of the first century, it will sometimes be difficult to understand the original meaning of the writers. Alfred Edersheim's *The Life and Times of Jesus the Messiah* is helpful in understanding the cultural context in which the Gospels were written. Groundbreaking (though controversial) work in this area of Scripture interpretation is being done through scholars such as James Dunn, N. T. Wright, and others.

History

Understanding the historical landscape in which the Bible was written is helpful to understand the meaning of texts and, more broadly, the *occasion* and *purpose* for each book of the Bible. For example, understanding Babylonian, Persian, Greek, and Roman history will enable us to more clearly understand the Book of Daniel. Understanding the messianic expectations of Israel when both John the Baptist and Jesus appeared to them enhances our understanding of the Gospels and the early church's wrestling to understand and explain who Jesus was and is. Sometimes a good Bible dictionary, such as the *New International Bible Dictionary*, or a Bible handbook, such as *Unger's Bible Handbook*, will help you to understand the Scripture in its historical context.

Geography

Knowing the places where the stories in the Bible take place can make the Scriptures come alive to you in a unique way. Pull out maps and photos of biblical geography to enhance your understanding and appreciation of your reading.

UNDERSTAND KEY PRINCIPLES

The plain-meaning principle

The Bible needs to be understood in its literal, most natural, and obvious sense—its plain meaning that lies right on the surface. Of course, the Bible does contain figures of speech and symbols, especially in apocalyptic literature, but even at these times the Bible is still communicating literal, objective truth.

As a general rule of thumb, the Bible communicates itself in very literal ways. Too often preachers and teachers will try to find the unique interpretation of a given text and end up confusing those they are teaching. The aim of good interpretation is not uniqueness. That sort of thinking is often pride rooted in a need to seem profound in front of others. Avoid this sort of biblical interpretation and motivation at all costs.

The historical principle

The Bible was written in a very specific historical context to a very specific audience over a fifteen hundred-year period. It behooves us to understand what the text meant to the people it was originally written to reach, despite the fact that we are so very far removed from the time in which it was written. Interpretation of Scripture continually finds itself in the tension between its *eternal relevance* and its *historical particularity.*

The grammatical principle

In order to accurately interpret Scripture, understanding the basic grammatical structure of each sentence and paragraph in the original languages is invaluable and necessary.

The inductive principle

The Bible interprets itself and does not contradict itself. Scripture is to be interpreted in light of itself in order to value its full meaning.

APPROACH PRAYER

There are three types of prayer: intercessory, supplicatory, and contemplative.

Intercessory prayer is when we stand in the gap and beseech God's hand for certain issues or people. These are prayers such as, "Lord, send revival to Somalia. Break through in power in that region." Supplicatory prayer is when we pray for our own immediate areas of need. For example, we might pray, "Lord, my car broke down. Would You provide me with a new one?"

And then there's contemplative prayer. Contemplative prayer, or mediation, is a type of prayer that involves slow, loving adoration of God through His Word. It is a type of prayer that is often overlooked, but it is the most intimate and illuminating. You could spend hours in intercessory and supplicatory prayer (and you should!), but if you skip contemplative prayer, your inner man will not grow to its full potential in the light and life of revelation of God. It is one thing to make a request, but it's quite another thing to adore. Contemplative prayer is when the fire of intimacy and hunger for God is kindled. It's when you come before God with no agenda and no requests except to encounter Him, and you gaze on His beauty, letting it strike your heart and awaken you.

I realize a lot of the words I'm using here are flowery and a bit vague: *gaze, behold, let His beauty strike your heart.* I know that will be a stumbling block for a lot of people. But I'm telling you, there is something so real, so life-giving, and so transcendent that happens when you come to God in meditation. Granted, it is a painfully passive type of prayer. It is so much easier to come to God with a list of requests and so much harder to be quiet and mull over a passage of Scripture, praying it back to God. It feels dumb, if I'm to be completely honest. It feels weak.

But as we've learned, we are in this inside-outside, upside-down kingdom of God, and the way He sets things up is not so that the strong and mighty may come to Him, but so that the hungry and thirsty, the weak and the broken may come. Contemplative prayer will confront your pride. It will confront your strife and your sense of wanting to prove something to God. But if you just keep at it, working it into your daily routine, I promise it will change your life, and you will experience the intimacy with God you have been craving all along.

Appendix C

THE PURITY COVENANT

HERE ARE SEVEN personal commitments you can make in your covenant to be holy before God in purity.

Commitment #1

> Confess your trespasses to one another...that you may be healed.
>
> —JAMES 5:16

I commit to refuse to participate in conversations that promote or joke about immorality. If I do speak in this way, I will confess to those I was conversing with that I sinned.

Commitment #2

I commit to wear modest clothing that in no way promotes sensuality. I will occasionally ask a godly believer who does not dress the same way I do if my clothing is too revealing (too tight, too short, etc.).

Commitment #3

I commit to confess each time I view pornography or have any sexual contact with someone not my spouse to the same trusted friend who embraces this covenant. I commit to register with the technology of choice that promotes the wisdom and safety of accountability, whether or not I struggle with pornography.

Accountability software. These programs track your Internet activity and send an e-mail to the accountability partner that you choose. If you uninstall the software, it triggers a report to your partner:

- www.covenanteyes.com
- www.x3watch.com
- www.integrity.com
- www.accountable2you.com

Web-filtering software. These programs will block sexual content from your computer:

- www.integrity.com
- www.intego.com (for Macs)
- www.cyberpatrol.com

Commitment #4

I commit to hold any confession of my friend's failure in strict confidentiality. If I do speak it to another, then

I commit to tell it to the one who confessed their sin to me. The one who breaks confidence should confess also to the one with whom he broke the confidence.

Commitment #5

If I repeatedly stumble in immorality, I will show the fruit of repentance by going with my friend to confess to the leadership of my church and then accept the boundaries they give me.

Commitment #6

> If your brother sins against you, go and tell him his fault between you and him *alone*. If he hears you, you have gained your brother. But if he will not hear, *take with you one or two more....* If he refuses to hear them, *tell it to the church.*
> —MATTHEW 18:15–17, EMPHASIS ADDED

I commit to share with the leadership of my church if my friend repeatedly stumbles in immorality. I will first tell my friend before sharing with a leader to convince him to go with me. I refuse to yield to unsanctified mercy that allows sin to increase in my friend's life.

Commitment #7

> Those who *continue* in sin, rebuke in the presence of *all*.
> —1 TIMOTHY 5:20, NAS, EMPHASIS ADDED

Above all things have fervent love for one another, for "love will cover a multitude of sins."

—1 Peter 4:8

I commit to follow through on the process of bringing those who continue in immorality to the appropriate discipline without offering unsanctified mercy. I will not seek to bring public shame to anyone who repents. I hope to never expose one's sin publicly, acknowledging there are many levels of discipline that do not require personal exposure.

NOTES

CHAPTER 1
THE MOST IMPORTANT QUESTION

1. A. W. Tozer, *The Knowledge of the Holy* (New York: Harper Collins, 1961), 1–2.
2. C. S. Lewis, "The Weight of Glory," in *The Weight of Glory* (New York: HarperCollins, 2001), 26.

CHAPTER 4
AN EXTRAVAGANT DEVOTION

1. Fifth Sense, "Psychology and Smell," http://www.fifthsense.org.uk/what_is_smell/psychology/ (accessed March 1, 2015).
2. Nate Saint, as quoted by Mission Aviation Fellowship, http://www.maf.org/about/history/nate-saint#.VNMrEVXF87Q (accessed March 1, 2015).
3. Amy Carmichael, *A Very Present Help: Life Messages of Great Christians*, comp. Judith Couchman (n.p.: Vine Books, 1996); Goodreads.com, "Amy Carmichael Quotes," http://www.goodreads.com/quotes/428784-the-best-training-is-to-learn-to-accept-everything-as (accessed March 1, 2015).

CHAPTER 5
THE ANCIENT DREAM

1. Goodreads.com, "Amy Carmichael Quotes," http://www.goodreads.com/

quotes/7595-we-profess-to-be-strangers-and
-pilgrims-seeking-after-a (accessed March 1, 2015).

2. "I Have Decided to Follow Jesus" by S. Sundar
   Singh. Public domain.

CHAPTER 7
A HAPPY HOLINESS

1. C. S. Lewis, *Letters to an American Lady*, ed.
   Clyde S. Kilby (Grand Rapids, MI: Wm. B.
   Eerdmans Publishing Co., 2014), 11.

2. John Wesley, *A Plain Account of Christian Perfection* (London: Epworth Press, 1979), 5.

CHAPTER 8
SINGING BACK THE KING

1. Global Missions Network, "Inspirational
   Quotes," http://www.globalmissionsnetwork.info/
   flquotes.html (accessed March 3, 2015).

2. John Piper, *A Hunger for God: Desiring God
   Through Fasting and Prayer* (Wheaton, IL:
   Crossway, 1997), 107.

3. Walter Wink, *The Powers That Be: Theology
   for a New Millennium* (New York: Doubleday,
   1999), 187.

4. John Piper, *Let the Nations Be Glad* (Grand
   Rapids, MI: Baker Academic, 2010), 35–36.

5. See legacy.joshuaproject.net.

6. George Otis Jr., *The Last of the Giants: Lifting
   the Veil on Islam and the End Times* (Grand
   Rapids, MI: Chosen Books, 1991), 261–264.

CHAPTER 9
FRIENDS OF THE BRIDEGROOM

1. Henri Nouwen, *The Selfless Way of Christ: Downward Mobility as a Christian Vocation* (Maryknoll, NY: Orbis, 2007), 28–29, emphasis added.
2. Charles Spurgeon, "The Friend of God," sermon 1962, http://www.spurgeongems.org/vols31-33/chs1962.pdf (accessed March 3, 2015).

EMPOWERED
TO RADICALLY CHANGE
YOUR WORLD

Charisma House brings you books, e-books, and other media from dynamic Spirit-filled Christians who are passionate about God.

Check out all of our releases from best-selling authors like **Jentezen Franklin**, **Perry Stone**, and **Kimberly Daniels** and experience God's supernatural power at work.

CHARISMA
HOUSE

www.charismahouse.com
twitter.com/charismahouse • facebook.com/charismahouse

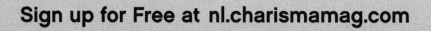